A veteran of Melbourne's underworld, Mick Gatto is one of the few survivors of Melbourne's Gangland Wars. Many of the victims were his long-time friends. Today the former heavyweight boxer runs Elite Cranes, a crane company that employs about sixty people, and Arbitrations and Mediations Pty Ltd, among others.

Tom Noble has been a journalist for more than twenty-five years, working mostly in newspapers. He is the author of the bestselling true crime books *Untold Violence*, *Walsh Street* and *Neddy*.

I, MICK GATTO

with TOM NOBLE

VICTORY BOOKS

VICTORY BOOKS
An imprint of Melbourne University Publishing Limited
187 Grattan Street, Carlton, Victoria 3053, Australia
mup-info@unimelb.edu.au
www.mup.com.au

First published 2009
Reprinted 2009
Text © Mick Gatto and Tom Noble, 2009
Design and typography © Melbourne University Publishing Limited, 2009

Pages 197–8: reproduced with permission from David Elias and *The Age*; pages 199–200: reproduced with permission from Gary Hughes and *The Australian*; pages 221–2: reproduced with permission from Mark Hawthorne and *The Age*.

Every attempt has been made to locate the copyright holders for material quoted in this book. Any person or organisation that may have been overlooked or misattributed may contact the publisher.

Typeset by Megan Ellis
Printed by Griffin Press, South Australia

National Library of Australia Cataloguing-in-Publication entry:
Gatto, Mick.

I, Mick Gatto / Mick Gatto; Tom Noble.

9780522857016 (pbk.)

Gatto, Mick.
Crime—Australia.
Criminals—Australia.
Gambling and crime—Australia.
Boxing—Australia.

Noble, Tom, 1964–

364.994

CONTENTS

Author's Note   vii

Preface   ix

1. A Death in Carlton   1

2. The Devil of South Melbourne   6

3. Going to Market   15

4. The Fight Game   23

5. Settling Down   35

6. The Other Business   43

7. Inside Time   52

8. The Two-Up   58

9. Playing Games   75

10. Crown Casino   87

11. The Union Business   91

12. Alphonse   98

13. Easy Money   107

14. The Wars Begin   116

15. Andrew   121

16. The Mediterranean   128

17. The Killing Fields   134

18. Graham   142

19. Hunting a Killer   148

20. No Comment   155

21. Revenge   162

22. Trial by Jury   173

23. Back in Town   184

24. Mario   190

25. Out of the Shadows   195

26. Rats in the Ranks   202

27. Melbourne's *Underbelly*   208

28. Problem-Solving   216

29. Last Man Standing   223

Acknowledgements   236

AUTHOR'S NOTE

Text that appears in square brackets in italics [*just like this*] through-out this book is written by Tom Noble, and provides background information for Mick Gatto's story.

PREFACE

This is the book I never wanted to write. But in the end, I had little choice.

The underworld, by its very definition, is a hidden world. And for most of my life, that's where I've made my living: out of the spotlight, under the radar, quietly doing my own little thing. But in 2008, the *Underbelly* television series propelled me into the limelight. I became a household name. I couldn't go out without being stopped in the street and asked for a photograph or autograph.

And with the success of the series, the people behind *Underbelly* said they were going to make a movie of 'The Mick Gatto Story'—with or without my input—so I knew I had to put pen to paper. I wasn't prepared to let them tell my story from underworld gossip, police files and court transcripts—I wanted it told as it really is.

I have done my best to be as honest as possible. There are some areas where I haven't been too specific, for obvious reasons. But beyond that, I've tried to give an open account of who I am, and how I got to where I am today. Most of the incidents in this book very few people knew about—until now.

I am donating a percentage of my royalties from this book, and any money from a film, to my favourite charity, the Royal Children's Hospital in Melbourne.

PREFACE

Looking back on my life, I certainly regret a few things I did, particularly when I was younger. If I had my time again there are a lot of things I would change. I definitely would have avoided going to jail and dragging my family through all that heartache. But you can't undo what's done. So here is my story.

Mick Gatto, August 2009

1

A DEATH IN CARLTON

My life changed forever the day I shot dead Australia's busiest hit man. It was Tuesday 23 March 2004, and Andrew 'Benji' Veniamin had dropped in at La Porcella restaurant in Carlton for a chat. We were standing in a back room, talking, when I told Andrew that he could no longer be trusted and I didn't want to see him any more.

My most vivid memory of that day is the look on his face. His eyes started spinning in his head and his whole expression changed. He went from Dr Jekyll to Mr Hyde. I couldn't believe it. I thought he was about to throw a punch. But he produced a gun. I don't know where it came from—the back of his pants, I think. I froze for a moment, then my boxing reflexes saved me as I pushed the gun away. It went *boom* straight past my head. I was convinced the bullet had hit me, but it hadn't; it just left gunpowder marks on my jacket. The noise was deafening.

I grabbed hold of his arm and turned the gun on him, squeezing his hand on the trigger, forcing him to shoot himself. And I kept squeezing. I had no idea how many shots were fired until much later. It was like one explosion after another, it was such a small room. Then I fell on the ground on top of him. He was gurgling and gasping, and I pulled the gun out of his hand. And as he lay there, blood bubbling out of his mouth, I knew he was gone.

In the months that followed, as I lay awake in my prison cell at night, that vision of him lying gurgling on the ground played over and over in my mind.

My plan that day had been pretty simple. I had to finish painting the garage door at home, meet a few people to talk business over lunch, then visit my cousin Roy at the Royal Melbourne Hospital (he had undergone surgery for cancer of the jaw). And that would be it.

I was running late so asked Charlie, who cleaned the spa at home, to finish the paintwork. I gave him $100. Then I jumped in the car and took off, picked up Ronnie [*Ron Bongetti, a long-time gambler in his mid-seventies and a close friend of Gatto*] and drove to La Porcella. It had become my 'office', a place where I'd meet builders, businessmen, union officials, friends. Most days I was there. I felt safe, because I was confident that the police had the building under surveillance, which was important. Three months earlier, my close friend Graham Kinniburgh had been shot dead outside his home. I'd made it my mission to find out who killed him. Six people had also been shot in the few months before Graham was killed, and word was out that I was next. And so I was carrying a gun again, or making sure one was nearby.

That Tuesday, I had a talk with a few people. There was a Chinese bloke who had some sort of asbestos problem in a building in Collins

Street, and he wanted me to talk to the union and limit the cost to fix it. There was a bloke named Geoff, a demolition-wrecker specialist. He's a rough diamond, been in and out of trouble all his life—drugs and things—and a mad punter. He called in to see me about a building dispute, then hung around and had a beer and something to eat. Lunch was fish and salad. It wasn't bad. I used to enjoy the food there. I met quite a few people that day and, luckily, most were too busy to stay for lunch, or they would have been caught up in what happened next.

I'd met Andrew Veniamin three or four years earlier. He was introduced to me as a man with a tough reputation—there were rumours he was a paid killer. Andrew was very ambitious, but had become increasingly erratic. Four days earlier he'd called me and we'd spoken for the first time in a while. I'd been trying to talk to him for some weeks, but his phone was always turned off. I wanted to know what he was up to, as he was closely involved with Carl Williams, and I suspected both of being involved in Graham's murder. As they say, you keep your friends close and your enemies closer.

At about 2 p.m., I phoned Andrew and, for the first time in weeks, his phone rang. And he answered.

'Are you around, mate?' I asked.

'Yeah, I am. I can be there soon.'

'All right', I said. 'I'll see you.'

He rocked up a few minutes later, came in and sat down. I was surprised he got there so quickly. There were six or seven of us around a table having lunch.

After a while, Andrew kicked me under the table and said, 'I want to have a chat'.

'Yeah, no worries', I said.

I stood up and started to walk into the street—it was a nice day outside—but instead Andrew headed to the back of the restaurant.

I'd often gone out there for a private conversation, and had been there before with Andrew, so I followed him.

When we got to the back room he turned to me. 'Look, I keep hearing that you still think I had something to do with Graham's death.'

'Well, I've got to be honest,' I said, 'that's what everyone's saying'. I also thought it myself—he may not have pulled the trigger, but I strongly suspected that he was somehow involved. I still do.

'But I wouldn't do that', he protested. 'You are a friend of mine, and I wouldn't harm anyone that's a friend of yours.'

I knew this was untrue, and so did half of Melbourne. Andrew was the hot suspect for several killings, including those of two of his closest friends, people he had grown up with. And I told him so. 'Dino Dibra and Paul Kallipolitis were your friends and you killed them.'

'They were fucking dogs, anyway', he said. 'They deserved it.'

And that's when I said, 'Mate, I don't want you in our company. You can't be trusted; it's as simple as that'.

I meant it. If you kill your lifelong friends, your childhood friends, how can you be trusted? Two guns had been emptied into Dino Dibra. Unbelievable.

That's when he blew up. 'Yeah?' he said, and took a step back.

Andrew was a lot smaller than me—he'd fought as a boxer and kickboxer in the lighter divisions—but he was quick. Luckily, I reacted in time, because there's no doubt he tried to kill me. If I hadn't reacted, I'd be dead, and he'd be doing twenty years' jail.

Moments later, as I walked from the room holding the gun, I tried to be as cool and calm as I could, but my heart was racing at 100 miles an hour. One minute I'd been minding my own business …

I walked back into the restaurant and grabbed the owner. 'You'd better ring the police and an ambulance', I said. 'He just tried to kill me and he's finished second best.' Then I washed my hands and got on the phone. I rang my lawyer first, who said he'd send someone straight down. Then I called my business partner Mat Tomas and told him what had happened. My two sons worked at our company, Elite Cranes, and I wanted to make sure they would be safe.

Then I called my wife, Cheryle, and told her to get our daughter to come home.

'What?' she said, then started screaming. 'What are you talking about?'

'Some rat's just tried to kill me, but he's finished up second best', I said. 'Don't worry about it; it'll be all right. Just grab the kids and go to someone's house and let things cool down.' Because I knew there'd be retaliation. I also knew there would be newsflashes on television, and that my family and friends would think that it was me that had been killed. I wanted them to know I was okay.

I still couldn't believe what was happening. I was sure then—and I still am—that Andrew did not come to La Porcella that day to kill me. When we went out the back, he left his car keys on the restaurant table. He simply came to ask me something, but one thing led to another; he lost his temper, and pulled a gun.

I knew I would be arrested and questioned so I sat around waiting for the police—and they started coming from everywhere. They were throwing all sorts of questions at me, and I said little. 'The only thing I'll tell you is it was self-defence', I said. 'He tried to kill me and he finished off worse. And I've got no other comment.' I could have left the scene but I had nothing to hide. As far as I was concerned it was a case of self-defence, and I was confident that once the police had done their forensic tests, I'd be released.

Instead, I was charged with murder and spent the next fourteen months in custody, unable to protect my family and friends as the killings went on.

2

THE DEVIL OF SOUTH MELBOURNE

My mother and father were both immigrants from Calabria in the south of Italy. My father was one of the first Italians to settle in this country, coming over in the 1920s. He was eighteen when he arrived, and had plenty of headaches. He did it tough, but got through all right. He worked in a range of jobs, from being a jackaroo up north to running an illegal gambling operation in Tasmania. He even spent a short time in jail: apparently some blokes mouthed off to him about being a wog and he chased them with a knife! In the 1950s he got involved in the markets in Melbourne, where he worked for more than fifty years—the rest of his life. First he was at the Footscray Wholesale Market, then he had his own stall at the South Melbourne Market.

He was a mad punter. He once won £4000 in the days when a good house cost £600, but he lost it again. He'd bet regularly at the market with another trader called Bob Hope. Sometimes they'd bet twenty cases of lettuces or tomatoes on the spin of a coin. Once they bet each other's truckload of fruit and vegetables—Dad won. He had an 'easy come, easy go' attitude with money, which is where I think I got it from.

My mother also arrived here when she was eighteen. My father was twenty years older than her, and she came over to marry him. Funnily enough, he'd sent her a photo of himself that was many years out of date. She still married him, though.

I was born on 6 August 1955 at Melbourne's Royal Women's Hospital. The story goes that Mum took a cab to the hospital but didn't make it to the ward in time, and I was born in the lift. I was the second child—I have an older sister, Rose; a younger brother, John; and a younger sister, Kathy. Home was 209 Cecil Street in South Melbourne, next door to the South Melbourne Fire Station. I didn't move out until I was twenty-one.

We spent a lot of time with others in the Italian community. Every week without fail there were one or two weddings, where there would usually be 1500 people, not to mention the three or four funerals a week—not that I went to many of those as a kid, but the parents would drag us along to the weddings. My father brought a few relations from overseas who lived with us until they found their feet.

I had a great childhood. I had a lot of free rein. I became very streetwise. In fact, I became a little villain. And that's probably why I'm so hard on my kids, reflecting back on it. Around the corner from home, in Park Street, was a row of Greek and Turkish clubs, such as Lesvos and The Canary, where men sat, talked and drank coffee. And inside were pinball machines, illegally rigged for gambling. I'm a compulsive gambler—I have been all my life—and once I discovered those machines (I was probably six or seven) I was hooked. I used to do anything to find money to play them: beg, borrow and steal. I was addicted to them.

I used to get the keys to the back of the machines, open them up and put my own credits on them. If I could, I'd take the money out and put it back in. We used washers instead of coins, and we'd drill holes in coins and put fishing line on them, so we could pull them out again and get more credits. We'd put wedges under the front legs of the pinball machines so the ball would run slower and we could guide it into the number we wanted.

I lost more often than I won. Once I did all my money when the ball just missed out on the number I wanted, and I lifted the machine and it went straight through the front window. The next minute all these Turks were running at me with knives—they were going to make shish kebabs with me, so I took off. [*A former neighbour said the young Gatto once walked up and asked to borrow a hammer, saying he wanted to knock in some nails. Instead, he walked up to a Greek club where they wouldn't pay his winnings, and used the hammer to smash the front windows.*]

When visitors came to our house, as soon as they walked in the door, my mother would grab their bags and hide them. We'd turn the house upside-down to try to find the bags and take their money. [*Another friend said that when the Gatto family came to visit, his mother would warn: 'Lock the doors to the bedrooms—the Gattos are coming!'*] One Easter, a woman came over and we grabbed her purse—it was full of money. I went to the shops and bought all the Easter eggs they had and shared them with about six of my mates. At a park across the road from the house, we began playing football with the eggs. It was great fun. But when the woman was leaving, she discovered her loss and told my parents.

Dad was a good man, but he had a short temper, and when we upset him he used to go off. That day he gave us a belting. He was wild, screaming and carrying on as he punched the shit out of us. We were beasts, and we deserved what we got.

The old women in the area used to call me the Devil of South Melbourne. It's very embarrassing, but it's true. I used to steal empty bottles from the back of shops, walk round the front and sell them. We even robbed the firemen next door. We used to break fire alarms or call from a phone box, and when they responded to the alarm we'd go in and take the money from their mess hall and put it into the machines. They suspected but never accused me.

One day I pulled the pay phone off the local laundromat wall and took it home to get the coins out. My father came in and caught me, and gave me the best belting.

I was about nine when I was caught in the back of the local cycle shop by a policeman called Brian Murphy, who took me to the police station and lifted me off the ground, hitting my head on the bookcase. I ran all the way home crying. The coppers were tough but fair.

Then there was a nearby warehouse we used to visit. One night the security guard chased me and my brother, yelling, 'Stop, or I'll shoot'. As we scaled the fence we heard shots—we jumped over pretty quickly.

On another occasion I broke into a house (aged about ten) and found this big elephant gun, and I ended up taking it home and putting it in our bedroom. Not long afterwards, my brother, John, got into a fight, and went home to get the gun to settle the argument! I didn't want him to take it and we were arguing outside the house when the police pulled up. 'Where did you get that?' they asked.

'We found it', we said.

And they took the gun off us. Not surprising, really.

There used to be a big department store on the corner of Bourke and Swanston streets called Foys. We used to go in and pinch stuff— we were villains—but one day we walked in and came across this great big tent, about 10 metres long, all rolled up and ready to go. So we put some brown paper around it; my brother jumped on one end, I jumped on the other and we marched out of the store with it. No one said a word. Two kids carrying a huge twenty-man tent.

We jumped on the Number 1 tram outside Foys, which took us all the way to our house. The tent reached from one door of the tram to the other.

At our stop, we got off and walked the tent across to the park opposite our house and put it up. We had a ball, until my father came out and saw us.

'Where did you get that?' he demanded.

'We found it.'

'Well, get home, now.'

So we did. And the next thing we knew, someone had pinched the tent. I was spewing. This beautiful tent, and we'd done all the hard yards.

We used to have fun exploring the neighbourhood. We regularly broke into the South Melbourne Town Hall and climbed up the inside of the tower to the top. And we would break into the building site near to home when they built the multi-storey Housing Commission apartments (not difficult). We'd climb as high as we could and hang upside-down by our feet from the top balcony, with our friends holding us. It was madness, really. Someone fell once and survived … until they moved him, and then he died.

We'd also get rolls of caps (a friend's mum worked in the factory where they made them for cap guns) and put them on train tracks, then sit in the tunnel and wait for a train. They would go off like a massive explosion and cause a horrific sound. It didn't cause any damage but gave us a laugh.

Our home was a couple of hundred metres from the St Vincent de Paul orphanage (it's gone now). About five hundred kids lived and went to school there—and I used to jump the fence and spend my time with those kids, take them food, play with them. I had a lot of friends in there. If I got caught I was thrown out, but I used to sneak back in. They told me stories of what the priests did to them; and then the bigger kids used to belt the little ones. A few of them had a pretty rough ride.

My brother, John, worked part-time at the market and started saving his money. He was a great saver, and built a big, strong money box that was in the shape of an anvil, with a slit on the top. This money box became a challenge. Every day I'd pull it out from under his bed, analyse it and try to get into it. I put wire down the hole—I tried everything—but I couldn't get any money out.

One day I was looking at the box again when I spied a knot of wood on the side. Using a hammer I hit the knot and it popped out perfectly. 'What about this!' I said as I put my hand in, took out a few notes and put the knot back in—a perfect fit. 'Who'd notice?' I thought.

This went on for a few weeks—he had a lot of money in there. And when I lost on the machines, then arrived back ten minutes later with more money, John would say, 'Where did you get that from?'

'Don't worry about it', I'd say.

He'd go home, check the box, and be happy I wasn't stealing from him.

When the notes ran out, I started taking coins. I ought to have been smarter and replaced them with rocks. But I didn't. He came home one night, lifted up his money box and realised it was too light. Next minute he'd broken it open and discovered the truth.

I was in the club playing a machine when John walked up behind me and broke a billiard cue over my head—twice. To this day he has never forgiven me.

Many years later when I ran the Two-Up, a bloke came in with a beautiful two-carat diamond. He wanted a couple of grand for it and I said to John, 'Run down the jewellers and get it checked out'—we had a mate down the road.

A while later he came back, saying, 'It's not much good; it's very ordinary quality. But I'm happy to buy it, even though it's not that good'.

So I let him buy it. I even lent him the money. It ended up being a top diamond that was worth a fortune. John evened up then—and since I broke into his money box he's evened up about a hundred times!

I got into a fair bit of trouble at school. And from pretty early on. One morning at primary school, Our Lady's in South Melbourne, I ran around with a mate, both of us holding a long piece of string. It somehow tangled round a kid's neck and the kid turned blue.

I don't remember much about the incident, except that every day before class we had to pray—and that particular day the prayers were focused on me and my mate, because we almost killed that kid.

I moved to St Peter and Paul's and, eventually, I got thrown out. The incident involved a new teacher, who was wearing a dust coat. For a joke, whenever the teacher went past, me and two friends, Mick and Mario, filled our pens from the inkwell and squirted him on the back—and he ended up with all this ink on his coat, soaked. Unfortunately, a couple of kids in the class gave us up, and we were in trouble.

The next day, there was a big assembly in what was known as Emerald Hall. There were hundreds of kids from the junior school, the high school across the road and the girls' school next door. I was sitting there when the penny dropped. The principal called us to the middle of the hall, where he pulled our pants down—with our undies on—and gave us six of the biggest straps across the arse. In front of the whole school I was humiliated, then expelled. I had big welts on the back of my bum and on my back, and couldn't sit down properly for two months. When my father saw my injuries, he went wild. He wanted to get a shotgun and kill them. I said, 'Dad, don't worry about it. It's my fault'.

My next school was South Tech (it's closed now), which was next to the Melbourne Sports and Aquatic Centre. My first day there was memorable because I had, literally, about twenty fights. The problem was, all these people had heard about me, it was halfway through the year, and I'd come from another school which was seen as the enemy. Everyone was having a go, calling me a 'wog', so I punched on with all of them.

I lasted only a few months at South Tech before I was expelled. I got caught smoking in the toilets, but that wasn't the problem. I can't remember what I did wrong, but I was called to the headmaster's office. And he kept poking me in the chest with his finger, really hard. I said, 'Stop doing that', and he kept doing it. It hurt, so I hit him. And ran.

To cut a long story short, the truant inspector—who'd paid several visits to my father over the years—went and saw Dad in the market. He said, 'Mr Gatto, whatever school your son goes to in Victoria they're going to throw him out. He's got to start work: his school days are finished'. So, in 1968, at the age of thirteen, I went to work.

3

GOING TO MARKET

My first job was stacking shelves at Coles. After two or three weeks, I was pushing a trolley around a corner when it tipped over by accident and the contents—disinfectants and chemicals—smashed. The supermarket promptly filled with a cloud of poisonous vapour. It was mayhem; no one could breathe. Everyone ran into the street. I was sacked. After that, I had a job with a panel beater for a couple of months, but I didn't really like it. So I finished up in the market, working for Dad.

The local coppers used to come to Dad's stall most weeks and get about $50-worth of food for nothing. They knew Dad well, because they'd dealt with me so often. Each time they caught me doing something, they would call my dad down to the police station and he'd give me a thump, then they would let us go. They'd be laughing. They got more satisfaction out of watching that than from charging me. And we'd get out the front and Dad would say, 'Are you all right?' That went on for a number of years. And the police also came for their free fruit and vegetables. If I was serving, I'd try to make sure everything they got was half-rotten.

I didn't last long with Dad, because we argued all the time. I think I brought the worst out in him, just broke his heart. I remember the first day I came home with a tattoo—I was twelve or thirteen—and he punched the shit out of me. The next day I went out and got another two. He gave it to me again. So I went and got some more. I was very rebellious. Instead, I worked for a Chinese bloke called Georgie Chen. I used to drive his truck to Footscray Market, then take the goods to South Melbourne Market. I was only thirteen, had no licence, but I used to love driving.

Georgie parked his truck in South Melbourne, and I could start the engine without a key. I used to take it for a run around Albert Park Lake with a couple of the boys. We'd fly around corners so quickly the truck would go up on its side. I nearly tipped it over many times.

One day I was driving back from Footscray Market fully loaded—Georgie was following in his car and was going to meet me at South Melbourne Market. Down Flinders Street, towards where the casino is now, there was a big roundabout. I went a bit quickly through it and the whole load fell off the truck onto the road.

The police were there. I had no licence, so I jumped from the truck and ran, leaving the entire mess behind. It wasn't far to the clubs just around the corner from home, so I headed there and started playing the machines. A little while later, out of the corner of my eye, I saw Dad run in carrying a tree branch, and he started giving it to me.

An old woman came over and said, 'Leave him alone'.

And Dad went to hit her.

'No, Dad, don't hit her; hit me', I shouted. And he did, demanding to know what I'd done.

I thought I was a great driver, but one day it went really wrong. I was driving up Dorcas Street past South Melbourne Police Station and towards the town hall when I spotted about ten coppers at the front of the police station. I don't quite know what happened, but I froze. The truck stalled, rolled down the hill, snapped a power pole in half and wiped out the whole area's electricity.

I jumped from the truck, ran down a laneway and hopped the fence into a woman's house, who had four or five kids. She let me stay there for about an hour, so I could sneak out later and go home. When I thought the coast was clear, I left—and the coppers grabbed me. I told them it wasn't me. So they took me back to the police station, gave me a bit of clip, then hung me out the first-floor window by my feet. I was screaming my eyes out because I thought they were going to drop me on my head.

Anyway, they called my dad, as usual. This time, though, I got a really good belt because it cost him about $1000, a fortune in those days, to get all the power put back on and fix the damage.

There were two market traders I knew who were bitter rivals. I used to get under their stands and pinch a box of apples or whatever from one of them, then sell it to his rival for a fraction of the normal cost. Next minute I'd pinch the other one's fruit and sell it to his rival. I successfully sold them each other's fruit for quite some time, and was never caught.

Once, one of them (who I'll call Jimmy) told me that his rival (who I'll call Billy) hid a big bag of money in his truck each morning.

I was still addicted to the machines, and this looked like an easy earn. The only problem was that everyone at the market knew me. So I got these two girls I knew to dress me as a woman—with a wig, make-up, dress, everything—and I went into the market dressed as a sheila. I walked up to this truck, broke the window and got the money bag, which had hundreds of dollars in it, and fled. I later gave Jimmy his whack.

I remember getting back to the market later that day and Billy came over, and he was white. 'You wouldn't believe what happened today. I got robbed! Someone robbed me and took my money bag.' Then he said it was a woman. 'This fucking moll was 6 foot tall, the fucking slut. People saw her do it.' Billy kept going, distressed. (It was a lot of money.) I couldn't control myself and laughed out loud. I even asked if she was good-looking. Billy never worked out it was me.

I loved the markets. I used to get to the wholesale market at four or five in the morning. I'd work in the retail market two or three days a week until perhaps 5 p.m. And I'd have every night off. The Footscray Wholesale Market didn't open until 6 a.m., although a lot of the growers would get there at 2 a.m. I used to turn up at about 5.30 a.m. to buy the goods for Georgie's retail stalls. After buying what we needed, I'd drive a little motorised scooter around, load it up, transport the fruit to the truck, then load the truck.

[*Melbourne's markets are rich in criminal history. In 1963 and 1964, a series of murders prompted allegations of Mafia involvement in the city's fruit and vegetable supply. Authorities arranged for an investigation by an FBI expert, who produced a detailed report on those involved and their roles.*] But I was just a kid and didn't think much about it, even though I knew quite a few of the people caught up in it. One was Mick DeMarti, a friend who was in partnership with my father for a while in the wholesale market. I used to push trolleys of fruit, and every time I went past his stand he'd say, '*Compare*, Mick, come here'. I'd go upstairs and he'd give me a couple of glasses of Scotch. I couldn't refuse him; he was a beautiful man. But after having a couple of Scotches, driving the motorised scooters I was nearly running people over. Mick was shot at his front door one morning in the 1960s. He survived.

The closest I came to serious trouble at the markets was when I was about fifteen. I was pushing a trolley loaded with fruit—I might have had a Scotch, too—past a row of tray trucks when I accidentally clipped a truck's back flap, which came off its hinges and fell on some bloke's toe. Two men there started screaming and yelling at me—then came running at me as if they were going to hit me, so I hit one and knocked him out. The other man started carrying on so I took off. The next day they came into the market with shotguns, looking for me: they were going to shoot me. And a couple of the old Italians heard about it and they went and grabbed them, and said, 'Hang on a second; you can't touch him'. Here I was, a kid, about to get assassinated for hitting a bloke on the toe.

About this time, I decided I really needed to learn some self-defence. I found a boxing gym and began training, but after a fortnight it closed. So I went wandering in North Melbourne and came across Kevin Watterson's gym. As I walked in, I noticed a Ford GT351 parked out the front, with machine gun holes in it. I thought, 'Oh my God, what's this?' It turned out the owner was a bouncer who worked at the Croxton Park Hotel, which was pretty rough in those days. He was always arguing with people so I think someone took their grievance out on his car.

Anyway, I walked in and talked to Kevin—and that was the start of a long association. As a teenager I'd started to grow—I'd been short and fat until then, but I shot up to be 6 foot 4 inches (193 centimetres). Dad was short and stocky, so I'm pretty sure I got it from Mum's side, as her brothers were all tall.

As a kid I always thought I was invincible, I really did. I thought no one could beat me in a fight and that I was better than everyone. I oozed confidence, and when I had a fight I always won. But when I started training and sparring, I got knocked around, whacked on the jaw, and began seeing stars. It quickly taught me a lot of respect, and turned me around. I went from being this cocky little villain to smartening up, respecting people and realising I was not as good as I thought I was.

I'm a firm believer that kids are a product of their environment, particularly of the people they run around with. Which is why I've always kept a close eye on who my kids associate with.

When I started fighting my demeanour changed, along with my whole attitude towards life. It didn't turn me into an angel—I certainly didn't back down from a fight if provoked—but I no longer went looking for trouble. It may also have saved my life. I'm convinced that if I hadn't taken up boxing I'd now be dead or in jail.

Even though at fifteen or sixteen I could have hurt my dad, I used to turn the other cheek when he hit me. I couldn't have struck him because of the respect and love I had for him. I copped it on the chin. I didn't like it, but I never, ever raised my hand to my father.

Around the corner from our house, in Park Street, was a low brick wall where a few of us used to sit some days and run amok. Now and then an older crowd came through from Port Melbourne. They were big and tough, and one, called Lindsay, was about 6 foot 6 inches (198 centimetres), a tall, wiry bloke who could fight like a threshing machine. They would walk up Park Street on the other side of the road from us and shout at me, 'How you going, you fucking wog?' I used to bow my head because they were four or five years older than me—and Lindsay could fight. I didn't want to get torn to pieces.

I got to about sixteen years of age and I met this girl I really liked, the first girl I was serious about. Her name was Christine. She was beautiful and I fell in love with her. (After we broke up she somehow became involved with the drug traffickers Kevin Barlow and Brian Chambers, who were hanged in Malaysia in July 1986. I don't know how she got tangled up with those reptiles, but they killed her. It was a tragedy.) One day I took Christine to a big Italian wedding and afterwards went to the Chevron Nightclub on St Kilda Road. I walked with her through the billiard room—and it was full of the blokes from Port Melbourne.

Lindsay looked up and called, 'How are you going, you fucking wog? What are you doing with her?' He looked at Christine. 'Do you know he's a fucking wog?'

I had to do something. 'Yeah?' I said. 'Come outside. I'll show you who's a wog.'

So I walked out ahead of him and, as I did so, he punched me in the back of the head. I was not impressed.

We got outside and I punched the shit out of him. I was so angry, I grabbed his head and smashed it on the bumper bar of a car. There was blood everywhere. His mates didn't stick their heads in because they knew he'd been giving it to me for years. The bouncers eventually came and stopped me.

I grabbed Christine and we left.

A few days later, we were sitting in Park Street and I saw Lindsay and his mates coming. I thought, 'Oh no, they're going to make salami out of me here'.

Anyway, he got near me and waved his hand in greeting. 'Mick, how are you, mate? How you doing?'

'Hello, mate, how are you?' I said. And we finished up mates.

4

THE FIGHT GAME

My first professional fight was on Monday 5 February 1973. I was seventeen and a half years old. I'd jumped straight to professional ranks simply because that was the gym I'd walked into: it trained professionals. If I had my time again, I would have fought first as an amateur—shorter fights, protective headgear and the chance to represent your country at events such as the Olympics. Instead, I was at Melbourne's Festival Hall fighting for a $30 purse. The money wasn't the incentive, though: it was the fitness and the glory, and the fact that I loved it.

I used to get up at 6 a.m. and run two or three times around Albert Park Lake. In the afternoon I'd go to the gym at about 4 p.m., spar a few rounds, do all the bag work and some more rounds, then the trainer would jump in and show me strategic moves. It was pretty strenuous stuff. My stomach was like a rock. In fact, I used to go to the South Melbourne Fire Station and stand against the fire truck, and they all used to glove up and hit me as hard as they could—and I'd laugh at them. I was really fit. I was supposed to be on a diet, but being a heavyweight it didn't really matter.

I quickly established a big following. Some nights Festival Hall struggled to draw a crowd, but when I fought there were firemen, friends from school and the orphanage, and hundreds of Italians from the markets who came to watch and cheer. They loved it. I think there was even a fight in the crowd one day, where someone was stabbed.

I was spending an increasing amount of time around St Kilda's discos and nightclubs, such as Mickey's Disco and Oscar's Nightclub. They used to have drag queens called Les Girls. I became friendly with a few of them and, to my embarrassment, they came to the fights. In among the old Italians and the boxing crowd would be these drag queens, in all their sartorial splendour, feathers everywhere, yelling and screaming and rooting for me. People would be looking round at them and I'd get that embarrassed. But it was great to have them there. It was quite a mixture of people and I always had strong support.

I don't remember much of my first fight, which I won on points in three rounds against Les Williams. My second and third fights were against Gary Remington—first time I beat him on points; second time I knocked him out. After the second fight I went out and sat in the crowd. My trainer walked past, and I looked up and asked, 'When am I fighting?'

'What do you mean?' he said.

'When am I fighting? When am I on?'

'You just knocked the bloke out', he said.

I didn't believe him. I'd obviously copped one in the head and had amnesia.

My fourth fight was against Wayne Windahl. He was a friend and was quite mad; in fact, he was the boy my brother had wanted to kill with the elephant gun. The bloke I was meant to fight didn't turn up, and Wayne, who was a champion from up the Riverina way, was the first emergency.

As we were walking into the ring together, he said, 'Let's just take it easy'.

We were getting only $10 a round, so I said, 'All right, no problems'.

The bell went, and the first thing he did was try to knock me out. Unfortunately for him, I ended up knocking him out.

I grabbed him after the fight and said, 'Mate, what were you doing? You said take it easy, then you tried to knock me out'.

He apologised. 'I just got excited. Sorry.'

We're still mates today.

My fifth fight was against Marc Ecimovic, a big Croatian boy. I was in tip-top condition. I remember his trainer came and saw me, and said, 'If you knock him down he won't get up again. He's like that; he won't get up'.

So with the first few punches I threw, I knocked him down, and I thought, 'Beautiful, the fight's over'.

Anyway, he jumped up.

The next minute, *bang, bang, bang*—I knocked him down again. I was very sharp and fit. And I was convinced that that was it—the fight was over; he was being counted out.

I don't know how it happened, but without me really seeing him he ran at me and clocked me with a big right hand, which stunned me. And my trainer, Kevin Watterson, because he was frightened I might get hurt (I'd had only a handful of fights) threw in the towel to stop the fight. It might have been the right decision by Kevin, but I was filthy because I thought I'd been led up the garden path about knocking Marc down. I was furious—I should have knocked him out easily.

I was on TV two or three times in those first fights. I even won the 'Fight of the Night' award a couple of times, which was handed out by a bloke called Knuckles. And I remember Merv Williams, the fight commentator on *TV Ringside*, saying of me: 'He's built like a Greek god, this bloke. Women chase him like bees to a honey pot'. Merv was right about that—women chased me. I also did my fair share of chasing. In fact, I became so keen on nightclubs and girls that I didn't box professionally again for almost a year.

When I started training at Kevin Watterson's gym, it didn't take me long to notice something unusual. Each afternoon, people would arrive and head upstairs. I was curious, and Kevin tried to keep me out, but that didn't last long.

Upstairs was the Two-Up, Melbourne's biggest illegal gambling den. Kevin was one of the partners, along with Lionel 'Nappy' Ollington, Ron Bongetti, Bruce Johnstone and Frank Borg. Two-up was the name of the wonderful game that was played at the club. It involved spinning two pennies into the air from a wooden board, or kip. Players would bet whether the coins would come up with two heads or two tails. If it was one of each, they'd be thrown again. It was that simple. The house made its money by taking a small commission on winning bets.

Before long I managed to get myself a job upstairs, working as a bender—someone who bent down and picked up the coins when they'd been spun in the air, yell out the result, pay the people who won, collect from those who lost, and take the house commission.

Bruce took a shine to me, and soon I was working with him as a starting price (SP) bookmaker. [*According to Johnstone, he and Gatto set up in a small office in Williamstown with two phones, and began taking big bets. Johnstone kicked the bank off with $10000. After two months they had turned it into about $30000, so gave themselves $5000 each as 'profit'. Their luck turned and the bank shrank, so Johnstone asked Gatto for some of the $5000 back—but he'd already gambled it all. 'From then on he was on wages.'*] Because Bruce was busy with the SP, he regularly arrived late at the Two-Up. He was meant to be there for a 3 p.m. start, but the last race wouldn't finish until about 5 p.m. Kevin used to give it to him a bit, saying, 'You have to be here on time; it's no good'. They were forever arguing, and that's when I saw the angle. I asked Kevin, my trainer, if he'd be upset if I approached Bruce about a share: if I ran the game before he arrived, could I take a cut in the profits? He had no problem. So I asked Bruce. We haggled about it, and settled at 10 or 20 per cent. I was in. And before long I was making good money.

Many years ago there were two different two-up games in Melbourne: Nappy Ollington's game and Billy Brewster's game. They were in opposition to each other, with a bit of friction over the years. Eventually Brewster died, and about forty years ago the two games ended up being amalgamated. Ron Bongetti, who had been involved in two-up for decades as part of Brewster's game, had one shift, and Nappy had the other. They used to alternate: one week one would go from 3 p.m. to 8 p.m. and the other would go from 8 p.m. until whenever; then the next week it would change around. And they shared costs.

While his roots were Italian, Ron was born in Australia and he was just a beautiful man, although he had a tough reputation. One evening, not long after I'd started, there was a disturbance at the end of the table, and Ron was arguing with two big blokes. One made his hand into the shape of a gun, pointed it at Ron and said, 'You're dead. I'm going to shoot you'.

I grabbed him and said, 'Pull up, would you?'

He said it again, so I whacked him and knocked him out. The bloke with him shut up pretty quickly.

'Have you got anything to say?' I asked him.

'No.'

'Well, grab your mate and get out of here.'

From that day onwards Ron became really attached to me, because I stuck my head out for him.

Another key person I met at the Two-Up was Brian Kane. [*At the time, Kane was Melbourne's pre-eminent standover man, and has been portrayed in a range of television shows, including* The Great Bookie Robbery *and* Underbelly 2. *He was shot dead in 1982.*] Brian used to call in to the gym a bit. He loved the boxing, and had apparently been a handy boxer in his day. He used to see a few of the fighters, and I got to know him and like him. He had a bit of character about him. He was good at what he did, was very smart—and had a lot of people terrified. He and his brothers were pretty strong. I knew him quite well, along with the younger brother, Muscles [*Ray*], and I met Les a couple of times. I never saw them stand over anyone, but they were getting paid protection in different clubs and they made sure things never went pear-shaped. They punched on with a lot of police in different nightclubs. There were lots of stories and rumours as I was growing up, but I never saw or knew about any of it.

Brian got a good feed out of the Two-Up: $1000 a week to make sure no one else opened up. And he had place cards put around everywhere, through the markets, the waterfront, the Two-Up and others. You had to pick so many winners in so many races to win the pool. They were lucrative for him. He also used to look after a few SP bookmakers [*and collected debts for them*].

One night there were a couple of blokes in a car outside the Two-Up with balaclavas and shotguns. They were going to run in. They actually grabbed me, because I knew them—I was only a bender at the time—and they said, 'We're going to come in and stick the joint up'.

I said, 'Well, Brian Kane looks after the joint. If you do that, be prepared to die'.

So they didn't. I pulled them up. And it probably saved their lives.

Not long after I began my professional boxing career, I was picked up by a security company to work as a bouncer. I avoided nightclubs and pubs, and worked only at outdoor concerts at places such as the Sidney Myer Music Bowl, South Melbourne Cricket Ground and Festival Hall. I did it to let my friends in for nothing; I could sneak fifteen or twenty people into a concert.

When I was about eighteen, I went out with a girl called Midnight. She was tough, with tattoos all over her. She could fight better than the men. I remember one Greek bloke tried to plum her up one night, and she went *whack*—knocked him straight out. She was a heroin addict, too. Some nights I'd take her out, she'd shoot up, and the next minute she'd be vomiting. As a kid I saw junkies shoot up in their eye, in their arms, and in the webbing between their toes and fingers. It's sickening: they run out of veins.

Midnight's ex-boyfriend was the leader of the Hell's Angels at the time, a bloke called Root Rat. Once he came up to me and said, 'I know you're taking Midnight out. I've got no problem with it, just do the right thing by her'. And we ended up as mates.

One night I was employed to do security for Suzi Quatro at Festival Hall. There were twenty or thirty of us on security that night, and there was an area in the hall full of Hell's Angels. They were playing up, throwing things, screaming and carrying on. And all the security blokes, including me, became very nervous. We thought we were going to be killed.

I'll never forget what happened next. This Hell's Angel walked down from the crowd—it was Root Rat.

'Mick, how are you? What are you doing here?'

'Oh mate, I'm doing security.' I said, 'Everyone's shitting themselves thinking something's going to happen'.

'Mick, leave it to me', he said.

He walked up to where they were carrying on, and everything changed. Suddenly the joint was quiet as a lamb: there wasn't a peep out of them. The head of the security company came over and asked, 'What did you say to them blokes?'

I said, 'I told them if they don't stop fucking around I'm going to throw them all out'.

He said, 'You're joking?'

'No, no, I'm telling you. I told them we'll throw them all out.'

I gained a lot of credibility from that, but the truth was that Root Rat respected me and pulled them all up.

Another night, although I don't remember this, I was working at the Sidney Myer Music Bowl. Chopper Read said I stopped a bloke hitting him on the head with a claw hammer during a brawl. And he's respected me ever since. [*Mark 'Chopper' Read is one of Australia's best known criminals, an artist and bestselling author whose life story was turned into a successful film.*] And I've often said, if I had known the way Chopper was going to turn out I wouldn't have stopped the bloke! But Chopper has mellowed and he's a different person to the one I had some trouble with in the 1980s. In fact, he recently gave me one of his paintings, which hangs proudly in our family home.

I never got into the pub scene. When I went to hotels in Port Melbourne and South Melbourne I'd see people who were friends punch on with each other, or stab each other. It was out of control. I thought, 'How could you do that to a friend?' So I stayed away.

Instead, I went nightclubbing. In fact, I went out nightclubbing most nights of the week, often after finishing work at the Two-Up. I drank a fair bit, mostly spirits, and smoked a lot—about eighty cigarettes a day—which wasn't good for the boxing training. I regularly went to Billboard in Russell Street, in the city. Friends from all walks of life used to mingle and catch up. It was a meeting place. Some nights there were ten of us; some nights there were fifty. We were all out for a good time.

One night after closing, the head of security—a bloke known as Ugly—came over, pulled out a gun and said, 'Have a look at this'. Me and some of the blokes I was with, we all pulled out our guns. (I'd started carrying one to protect the cash at the Two-Up.) There was no one in the club, so the next minute we started target practice on the lights and disco balls. Ugly fired the first shots, and soon it was like the OK Corral, shots going off everywhere. It was drunk and stupid, really. No one was hurt, but we made a mess. The next day, the owner arranged for new disco balls and had the bullet holes patched up.

Another night I was in St Kilda at the front of the sea aquarium with my brother, John, and a few mates. All of a sudden we got in a fight with all these Turks. It was a spur-of-the-moment thing. John was pretty hot-tempered and started punching on with these blokes, and they pulled out knives. A blade went straight through John's arm—in one side and out the other. We jumped in our car and another knife came straight through the car door. These Turks were all mad. And then the police arrived and arrested everyone. (John needed a couple of stitches, but was okay.)

The Turks that stabbed my brother were taken to St Kilda Police Station and we went there to identify them. As one of my mates walked out from identifying those involved, I asked him which of them had stabbed John. 'The one in the middle.' So I went in, and I saw him on the other side of a table. I've never been too angry in my life, which is good; you can push me a fair bit. But once you push me over that limit I sort of lose it. That night I was furious—that knife could as easily have gone through John's heart. And when I lose it I'm capable of doing anything. When a policeman asked me which one did it, I just jumped over the table and started giving it to this Turk. The police tried to stop me, and they got hit too. I didn't mean to hit the police. I was just that angry.

The next minute I was locked up in a cell next to these rats, and we were all throwing abuse. I was charged with assaulting police, and when it got to court, I got the heavier penalty. They got a minimal fine. Some justice.

I used to drive an orange Monaro, a big V8. I loved that car. One evening about thirty of us were down in Port Melbourne, flying around the streets, racing each other. A few of the boys had hotted-up cars and we used to show off a bit.

I was closely following behind this panel van—funnily enough we weren't speeding, and I was certainly sober—when all of a sudden the van veered out really quickly, and then I hit something.

I looked in my rear-vision mirror and said, 'What was that?'

'I think it was a rubbish bin', said someone in the car.

I looked back and said, 'No, I think it was a person'.

I slammed on the brakes and ran back, and this bloke was lying dead on the road. I freaked out. Some of the people there who knew me came over and put the wind right up me.

'Oh, mate, you're gone.'

'You'll get charged with murder.'

'Mate, you'd better go.'

I was eighteen and terrified. But what saved me was that I ran across to a phone box and rang an ambulance. Then I went back to the scene and, with everyone saying, 'Mate, you're in trouble, you'd better go', I jumped in the car and took off.

For several months nothing happened. Then, one day, the police seized my car. They asked me what had happened, and I owned up. In short, the bloke was very drunk, dressed in dark clothing, it was a dark night, the car in front of me had just missed him and unfortunately I collected him. When it got to court I was fined $200 and lost my licence for a year.

It turned out the dead man was a respected member of the Painters and Dockers [*a powerful union, especially in the 1970s, with strong criminal connections. Some years later a wide-ranging royal commission probed its illegal activities*]. I'd stopped working at the markets shortly after the accident (I was doing well enough at the

Two-Up), and a few of the Painters and Dockers thought that I'd been paid to run the bloke over—that it was a professional hit. And pretty soon I heard that there was a contract on me. It might have been just a rumour, but I took it seriously. I approached Brian Kane at the gym and mentioned it to him. He said he would look into it. In turn, he told the Painters and Dockers that it wasn't intended: it was an accident. And with that, they agreed they had no problem with me, and left it. Thankfully, Brian Kane halted what was the first contract taken out on my life.

5

SETTLING DOWN

One of my favourite nightclubs was Peanuts, in the city. I loved it. Aged in my early twenties I was an imposing-looking bloke. I had a great body, and I was very, very fit. I would wear overalls with no shirt on underneath. And I used to get a different girl just about every night—so much so that there was plenty written about me on the walls of the girls' toilets.

One night I noticed this Australian girl, blonde, who watched the band and didn't mix with anyone. She was never up dancing. She stood out in the crowd, and was really elegant. She didn't play the field and go out with different blokes like many of the girls there. I was intrigued. I made a few attempts to talk to her, but she didn't want much to do with me. She thought I was up myself. I'm not surprised: she used to see me sitting on the stairway leading down to the dance floor and there'd be a girl on each knee. And all this nonsense was written in the toilets about me. She knew my reputation and veered away from me. It was a challenge to get her and I had to work really hard.

Eventually, I got her around and Cheryle and I started seeing each other. And because I'd lost my licence (after the Port Melbourne accident), she used to drive me everywhere. We got on really well and developed a great friendship.

We were at her flat in Kew when I proposed to her. There was nothing romantic about it; I just asked. I didn't think she'd say 'yes', to be honest. And when she said 'yes' I was a bit taken aback.

So I went and spoke to her parents. Her dad was fine, but her mum said to her, 'He's a lovely boy, but why are you marrying him?'

My dad was fine, too, when I went with Cheryle to tell my parents. 'If you are happy, I'm happy', he said.

But my mother wasn't happy. 'This must be a joke', she said. She wanted me to marry an Italian girl. But it didn't take Mum long to fall in love with Cheryle too.

Put simply, it was the best decision of my life. She's a great woman, she really is. She is beautiful and intelligent, and everyone loves her. She can't do enough for people, is always the first one to help, and never complains. She has been my backbone for a long, long time. I love her.

My buck's night was at a nightclub in St Kilda. We hired the top floor and I got extremely drunk. My mates organised some strippers, who took my pants off and put all sorts of stuff over me—sugar, alcohol and God knows what. It was quite embarrassing being stripped naked in front of all my mates, but there was no harm done.

We were married at the Park Orchards Chalet on 25 February 1978, near where Cheryle's parents lived. I was twenty-two and Cheryle twenty-four. There were about two hundred people at the wedding, which was big by Australian standards but not big in the Italian community. My sister, for example, had 1500 people at her wedding. But it was a great wedding, and we had a great night. My best man was Ange, who remains one of my closest friends today.

Funnily enough, Ange and another friend, Tino, also met their wives at Peanuts. We sometimes joked to our wives about whether we should go and burn the place down!

Our honeymoon was on Queensland's Gold Coast. My trainer, Kevin Watterson, had a magnificent property by the beach and he offered us the use of it. We stayed on the bottom floor, while upstairs lived The General—an old bloke famous in the underworld and the gambling world—and his wife, Kit. The General was a very big tipster, and people used to ring him from all over Australia to get a set of tips. He did his own research on horses and had his own contacts. His tips were pretty good. Kevin let him live there for nothing, and he stayed there for many, many years.

When we got back to Melbourne, we moved into a house in Thomastown, sharing with my brother, John, and his wife, Debbie (they later separated). Being married slowed me up a lot: no longer could I go out and party all the time; I had someone to answer to. But I still went out punting, gambling, working at the Two-Up, and sometimes I'd disappear from home for a couple of days. Cheryle was never too happy about it, but that was just me. It had been like that before we married.

One night she complained to her father, 'He's never home'.

And he said, 'Well, you made your bed; you've got to lie in it. He was like that before you met him. A leopard never changes its spots'. Her dad was a good bloke.

During our first year of marriage, we got lucky. My brother, John, best man, Ange, and I bought a Tattslotto ticket. We won—the first-division pool was about $300 000, an absolute fortune then. We were celebrating and carrying on. That night I gave my car and stereo away to a couple of friends, I was so excited. But the following Monday, it turned out that there were quite a few winners. We finished up with about $20 000 each, which was still a lot of money, but not what we'd expected.

I redeemed my car and stereo because there were so many winners. But it did give us a great start, and we bought a block of land in Wheelers Hill and started building our first home.

Also in our first year of marriage, Cheryle fell pregnant. On 23 February 1979—Saint Michael's Day—our first son, Michael, was born. I was at the birth, and was thrilled. He had a mop of curly black hair and a dark complexion (our other children were all born bald and had a fair complexion).

By this time, we'd moved into our home at Wheelers Hill. It was a fair drive from the city, so I decided to stay with a friend in Port Melbourne while Cheryle was in hospital in East Melbourne. Two days after Michael was born, the phone rang. I was asleep on the couch. It was for me.

'Mr Gatto, it's Doctor Smith from the Mercy Hospital. I've got some very bad news for you.'

'What's happened?'

'Your son has just died.'

I blew up. 'Is this some sort of fucking joke? Who is this? Why are you doing this?'

He said, 'No, I'm serious. I'm Doctor Smith, and I regret to inform you your son has died'.

I jumped in the car with this mate of mine from Port Melbourne and we drove to East Melbourne in no time. I was overtaking traffic, and the police saw me and gave chase. They had their siren going, but I wouldn't stop. I pulled up at the back of the hospital and I jumped out—and the police leaped out with their guns. I turned to them and said, 'My son's just fucking died; leave me the fuck alone'.

They backed off, said they were sorry and left, which was good of them. And I went and saw Cheryle, who was devastated. We were both devastated.

Afterwards, I walked down to the basement of the hospital, and went and saw my son. Michael was lying there, tiny. He was all purple, like he'd been choked. He'd just stopped breathing. It shattered us—a perfectly healthy baby and they couldn't explain how he died, except to call it a cot death. It was really, really hard at the time. We even talked nonsense about ending our own lives, we felt so empty.

One strong memory I have from that time is the generosity of Charlie Wootton. Soon after Michael died, I got a message that Charlie wanted to see me, so I went to visit him in St Kilda. And he handed me a wad of money, about $3000. 'That's to help bury your son.' I had no money at the time and I've been forever grateful to Charlie. It paid for the whole funeral. [*Charlie Wootton is a well-known figure in Melbourne's illegal gambling scene, having run clubs around St Kilda for many years. His clubs, like almost all of the city's illegal gambling, closed down in 1994 when Crown Casino opened.*]

On 24 June 1980, our son Damien was born. I was deeply worried that he would die, like Michael. Every ten or fifteen minutes at night I'd be in there checking him. We had monitors in the room to listen to his breathing. And I've been that way with all of them, because the only thing in life that really bothers me—and I can handle anything—is when my kids get sick. That's the time I go to water. And they've all been sick and been to hospital. Damien and Sarah (born in 1983) both suffered from febrile convulsions. Their temperature would get really high, they'd collapse, swallow their tongue, convulse, go blue.

The first time Damien had a seizure he was about two. He was standing talking to me and Cheryle when all of a sudden he fell straight on his face. I thought he was joking. I grabbed him and the next minute he was blue and had stopped breathing. I picked him up and ran next door, where our neighbour gave him heart massage and mouth-to-mouth. Damien started to breathe a bit; an ambulance came and they took him to the Royal Children's Hospital.

My youngest son, Justin, was born in 1985. He was two months premature, a tiny little thing. They didn't give him much chance of surviving, but he pulled through.

Damien, Sarah and Justin are all adults now—Damien has his own son, called Dominic—and I'll be forever grateful for the work of the staff at the hospitals, particularly the Royal Children's Hospital.

When I started going out with Cheryle, I was still boxing professionally. I even had a fight after we got married. But I never gave my career the attention I should have.

I was almost nineteen when I had my second series of fights: two bouts at Festival Hall. I lost the first and won the second in a knockout. But the dedication I'd shown in my first five fights was rapidly slipping. I was going to nightclubs, drinking, chasing girls. I was getting easy money from the Two-Up. I was sidetracked all the time, and lost the *hunger*. I used to smoke before a fight, and my trainer, Kevin Watterson, would go berserk.

But Kevin still thought I was 'the great white hope'. At one point he opened a gym at his home to train me on my own. But I'd have a fight, then give it away—it used to break his heart, the poor bugger.

My second-last fight was on Wednesday 9 March 1977, at Festival Hall. It was the main event, and I was twenty-one years old. At that time, professional boxing in Melbourne was struggling to pull a crowd of a few hundred to a midweek fight. That night there were 1500 people, of whom about 1400 were Calabrians from the markets!

I'd had a three-year break before the fight, and I'd never fought more than three rounds. This was a ten-round fight. This jump in distance, after such a long time off, was unheard of for a professional boxer. But it's what happened to me. And going the distance—being able to fight for the whole ten rounds—meant more to me than winning the fight.

In the end, it went all ten rounds. I have no memory of the last round, I was so exhausted. But I got there. I lost in a split decision, but I should have won. Reno Zurik, a champion from New South Wales, was very fit, very quick, and I couldn't catch the bastard: I had to run around the ring chasing him. But when I did hit him, he went flying—I knocked him down twice in that fight and he was gone for all money, but somehow he managed to get back on his feet.

I remember getting $300 for the fight. I fought my guts out for ten rounds, only just got beaten in a split decision, and that was my reward. The next day I went to the Two-Up and turned the $300 into $2000—I thought, 'This is easier than fighting', so I gave boxing away.

But Kevin used to get in my ear about having a rematch against Reno Zurik. He was persistent, even after I got married to Cheryle. And in the end, I gave it one more go. I was billed as 'The Italian Stallion', and there was a huge promotion for the fight, which was held in Griffith. My father-in-law came to that fight, as did many others from Melbourne. One group hired a plane and flew twenty people up.

It was the same result—I chased him around the ring trying to hit him, and lost in a split decision. (Later I became mates with the referee, and I asked him why he hadn't awarded me the fight. He said, 'Mick, I didn't know you then. If I had known you, I would have given it to you. There was nothing in it'.)

I had no more professional fights after that, although there were a few possibilities. At one stage I started training to fight Dave Russell, who'd won a world title. I was getting very fit, but then Dave defended his title and lost it.

Jeff Patterson, a fight promoter and friend, set up a deal for me to fight Tyrell Biggs in the United States as part of a five-fight deal. He said that if I beat Biggs, I could become a millionaire. But I turned it down. [*Biggs went on to win an Olympic gold medal in 1984 and challenge Mike Tyson—unsuccessfully—for the professional world heavyweight title. He later became a tragic figure, affected by drugs and alcohol.*]

Later, I looked at doing a promotional fight to raise money with 'Aussie' Joe Bugner. Bugner is a giant of a man: his hands are twice the size of mine. It would have been some fight. But that deal didn't come off either.

In many ways, I'm glad I gave boxing away. I had nine professional fights and had a great time. I've seen many people who kept going and didn't know when to stop, and they've been badly affected by the fight game. Because win, lose or draw, in a fight, you still come out hurt.

Not long after I stopped boxing, Kevin, my trainer, died. He had a crook heart, and used to defy the doctors, who told him he couldn't train. One day he had an operation and they gave him the all-clear. For the first time in his life he had a green light to do whatever he wanted. It wasn't long after that he was training in the ring when a fighter called Stan punched a pad which hit Kevin in the chest, and Kevin just died—his heart stopped. Stan, who was a great prospect, gave boxing away after that.

6

THE OTHER BUSINESS

Working at the Two-Up gave me an introduction to a new world. When I first met Kiwi Dave, he was wearing diamonds and gold all over him, driving a sports car. He was a really nice bloke. I was quite ambitious and, after a while, I said to him, 'Whatever you do, mate, I wouldn't mind being half in it'.

'Well,' he said, 'come with me'.

What I didn't know was that Kiwi Dave was on the run from the police. Not only that—he was New Zealand's most wanted man. The police had been trying to catch him for years, but he had this unbelievable sixth sense. The cops would raid where he was staying, but Kiwi Dave would have left moments before. And he would taunt the police. The coppers would burst in and Kiwi Dave would have left a note on the pillow, asking them to forward correspondence to a post office box in Zanzibar, and the like. These stories made it into the papers at the time. It turned out he was wanted over a big armed robbery in New Zealand, and the only witness against him was an elderly woman. But, try as they might, the coppers couldn't catch him. He was one step ahead of them for many, many years.

My first job with Kiwi Dave was at a house in Toorak that he'd been watching for a while. We went there and he turned off the alarms—he showed me how to do that—and I stayed at the front door as the nit-keeper [*lookout*]. He had a look around and opened the safe, which had a heap of diamonds in it. We finished up with a pretty nice earn each. Before long, Kiwi Dave was teaching me the ropes—and soon I was cutting safes open and turning off alarms.

Kiwi Dave had a habit of going into houses while people were asleep in bed. I hated that. I did it a couple of times with him, but stopped. It just wasn't my cup of tea. I was very uncomfortable doing it, and used to think, 'What if it was *my* mother who was asleep?' For Kiwi Dave, though, it was a breeze. But when he first went into a house he went straight to the cupboards to have a look at the size of their shoes—if they had large shoes he'd be really careful, because it meant they were big.

On occasions, the people in bed would hear him. They'd say, 'Is that you, Jamie?'

And he'd flush the toilet and say, 'Yes, Dad'.

And they'd go back to sleep. Just a normal reaction.

But one night he was in a house and the bloke woke up in the bedroom and said, 'Is that you, Buster?'

'Yes, Dad', said Kiwi Dave, flushing the toilet.

There was a pause, then a voice said, 'Buster's a fucking dog!'

The bloke jumped out of bed and gave chase, but Kiwi Dave had worked out his exits. He got away.

One afternoon, Kiwi Dave and I were pulled over by police in Beach Road, Albert Park. I won't mention the names of the police; suffice to say they were a couple of colourful coppers. One jumped from the car pointing a gun, shouting, 'Police! Don't move!' Then he saw it was me. 'Mick, I'm sorry, I didn't see you.' He put the gun away and kept apologising, 'I'm sorry, Mick'.

They turned the car upside-down and didn't find anything. But we were near Kiwi Dave's apartment, and they wanted to go up and have a look around. We went in, and they found a heap of fur coats, jewellery and other things that didn't belong to him.

'Look', said Kiwi Dave. 'I'll do you a deal. You keep all the stuff you've found here, and we'll just forget about it.' And that's what happened. They grabbed all the gear, took off, and that was the end of it.

Not long afterwards, Kiwi Dave needed to sell a big parcel of jewellery—he used to build it up from a few jobs, then, once he had enough, sell it to a fence [*dealer in stolen goods*]. He began talking to Black Jake, who bought and sold hot things—but Black Jake was also a police informer. They arranged to meet, and Kiwi Dave turned up in his sports car—and the police promptly blocked off both ends of the street and arrested him.

The police didn't know who Kiwi Dave was until they ran his fingerprints and found out he was the most wanted man in New Zealand. So they locked him up and sent him back to New Zealand.

I was filthy on this Black Jake, who I didn't know. There were only two people who had known where that meeting was going to be—and it wasn't Kiwi Dave who told the police.

Not long afterwards, I was at the Ivy Nightclub and I could hear this bloke at the bar, really boisterous—yelling, screaming and carrying on. He was with a couple of Croatian blokes I knew, and they came up and said hello.

'Hey, Mick', said one of them. 'Do you know Black Jake?'

I looked at him. 'You're Black Jake? You set a mate of mine up, Kiwi Dave.'

He put his drink down. I could see he was going to have a go at me, so I got in first and knocked him out. The bouncers then threw him out.

Kiwi Dave, meanwhile, was back in New Zealand. But while he was on remand, this poor elderly witness died of natural causes, so the whole case against him collapsed. They had to drop the charges and release him. Kiwi Dave came back to Australia, and he became a fight promoter and entrepreneur. He certainly doesn't steal any more. He lives in Queensland and does quite well for himself, and we are still good mates to this day.

I first came across Alphonse Gangitano at Mickey's Disco in St Kilda. We were about the same age and got on well, and before long we ran around a bit together. He was always a hot head—he wouldn't take a backward step to anyone—but he was a good kid when he was young. He changed a lot when he got older.

By the early 1980s, Alphonse had developed a big reputation for taking on off-duty coppers. [*In inner-suburban police stations, warnings were put up for staff about Alphonse and his crew. They would target two or three off-duty police drinking at a nightclub, then one of Alphonse's crew would provoke a fight, by spilling a drink or making a remark. Once the off-duty police made a move, Alphonse's crew would step in en masse and beat them mercilessly.*] Unfortunately—and unfairly—I got a reputation for that, too. Nine times out of ten, when Alphonse was involved in a shooting or a fight, the police would put me there. They'd say, 'He was in the company of Mick Gatto'.

It was rubbish. Alphonse had his own crew, but every time there was trouble the police would throw me in as well. Years later, different police would say, 'You were there, weren't you?' And I wasn't. I was home in bed. I was never part of it. But some of the mud stuck and I ended up with a reputation.

I did get in trouble with Alphonse one night, though, and it almost cost me years of my life. How we got away with it, I still don't know. Alphonse and I arrived at a St Kilda nightclub pretty drunk. There were about three or four hundred people waiting to get in, and we walked straight up to the front door.

The bouncer looked at Alphonse and said to him, 'You can't come in, mate, you got a tracksuit on'.

So Alphonse pulled a gun out and whacked him on the head.

And then this bloke came over and starting pointing at us and arguing. I found out later he was a cab driver who didn't like the police, and he thought we were coppers standing over the doorman. He should have minded his own business. I was pretty drunk and I hit him, and he went flying. He landed on the pack rack of an old MG, which broke off. So this bloke picked up an iron bar from the pack rack and tried to hit me with it. I put my hand up and fended it away, pulled out a gun and let a shot go. Thank God it missed. It went straight between his legs.

I looked at my hand, and it was chopped up and bleeding. I thought I'd shot myself, but it was the iron bar that had done the damage.

At that point, Alphonse ran up and stuck his revolver in the taxi driver's stomach and pulled the trigger. Revolvers don't jam, they don't miss, but somehow nothing happened.

We took off, and drove to a hospital to get my hand looked at. The doctor was stitching up my hand when the police came running in. They grabbed us, threw us in a divvy van and drove us back to the city.

Alphonse and I were put into a line-up and the taxi driver was asked to identify those who had attacked him. The police were looking pretty confident. This was their chance to lock up Alphonse and me. The taxi driver walked along and stopped in front of me—his head was pretty battered—and carefully looked me up and down. Then he continued walking along slowly and did the same thing to Alphonse. Police confidence quietly rose.

When the taxi driver reached the end of the row of the dozen or so blokes, he turned to the police and said, 'They're not here'. You could just about hear the jaws of the police hitting the ground. I'm convinced the taxi driver knew it was us and recognised us. I later found out he simply didn't like the police.

The next day we went back to the nightclub and a bouncer gave us the bullet from Alphonse's revolver. He said, 'Are you looking for that?' Apparently the gun had just been oiled and somehow, as the chamber turned, the bullet fell out. It should be impossible, but it happened.

That incident cured me of a lot of things. In reality, Alphonse should have killed the bloke and we both should have got twenty years' jail. It was my fault as much as his—I can't blame him—but from that day onwards I said, 'That's it'. I stopped running around with him and ran my own race.

While Kiwi Dave was the best at sneaking into houses while people were asleep, Graham Kinniburgh was a master at opening safes in offices and factories. I had the greatest admiration for Graham's professionalism—and he would be rolling in his grave if he knew I was telling stories about him, so I won't be too specific. He was tied up in the Magnetic Drill Gang [*an infamous group of robbers who netted millions of dollars in the 1970s*]—that's been documented, so I'm not speaking out of school. He was also a father-like figure to me, and taught me a lot over the years.

Graham knew every safe. One night I walked into a nightclub with him—with the nightclub going full swing—and we went to the office area. 'Watch this', he said, and turned the dial on the safe, and the door opened. It was unbelievable, brilliant.

Most of the jobs we pulled were at night. There was a fair bit involved: you had to work out how the alarms were monitored, how to turn them off, and how to wait for any watchman to come and check. Sometimes a job would be a bit more complex. We might break into someone's house at night and, while they were asleep, steal their keys. We'd get the keys copied, then return them before the person woke up, so they were none the wiser. Later, when a robbery took place, police would suspect it was an inside job.

If a building had high-level security, we'd try to find another way. For example, a jewellery shop might have sophisticated alarms and security to protect the safe holding the stock. But going through a wall from the next-door building and cutting open the *back* of the safe was a way to circumvent that.

At one point, new floor safes were brought into the country and they were impossible to crack. They had a chute at the top that you put money in, but without opening the safe, you couldn't get the money out. The answer? The crew would pour water down the chute and wait until the safe filled up and the money floated to the top, then pull it out with a wire, note by note.

I also worked with another crew, who I won't mention by name. In fact, I effectively worked as a freelancer, mostly keeping watch and listening to a radio scanner for police traffic. Sometimes I'd climb into buildings like a cat burglar ('Gatto' means 'cat' in Italian)—I was very fit then and not worried about heights. It was fun, a challenge, and exciting, and I never hurt anyone. Looking back, though, I'm not especially proud of stealing from people. The takings varied—it could be $2000 or $20 000—but unfortunately I'd quickly use it up on gambling.

There weren't many skilled safe-breakers, and some police had an idea what I was up to. A couple warned me to be careful. Then one day, a senior policeman I knew quite well came to my house. 'I like you', he said. 'I'm advising you to stop what you're doing. You're under surveillance.' Of course, I didn't listen. It turned out the police had a surveillance crew on me and a couple of others. They'd obviously heard on the grapevine what we were doing.

This particular day they were following us, but they lost us. The job was a golf course, where we successfully turned off the alarms and opened two safes. Four of us were involved, and two went one way, and, with a friend, Serg, I went the other. We pulled up at a house in Brighton where my car was parked, and the police pounced. In the boot of our car was a heap of alcohol and a bit of money from the golf course. While I was sitting in the divvy van, the police took my runners and went back to the golf course, where they put my footprints all over the place, to cement their case and ensure there was enough evidence. All's fair in love and war. And in the long term they did me a favour.

They also had a pretty good idea who else was on the job—they even mentioned one of their names during the interviews. I said nothing and they couldn't pin it on either of them. After a night in the cells I was charged and bailed. I realised that unless I was lucky, I'd be going to jail.

7

INSIDE TIME

Soon after I was bailed, Cheryle asked me what had happened. I told her I'd had nothing to do with the burglary—I'd met some bloke who gave me the alcohol and I got caught with it in the car. I told her the police had set me up. That was my story and I was sticking with it.

In those days it was the golden rule among us blokes (and still is)—don't tell your wife or girlfriend anything. Why let them implicate you later if the relationship breaks down? It was also for their own protection: what you don't know can't get you into trouble. Cheryle had no idea what I'd been up to.

I knew it was very important to get a good lawyer, someone who was switched on and knew what to do. I've learned over the years that cost is not important—you don't want to be robbed, but it's vital to have the best legal advice possible. Through word of mouth I came to a lawyer I'll call Bob, who ran the case.

That experience left me with a bad taste for solicitors, and my opinion hasn't changed much. (There are exceptions, such as Robert Richter—more on him later.) A lot of solicitors are like scavengers. We need them, but many of them are interested only in the money. They work on other people's miseries, don't have their clients' interests at heart and stretch things out to suit themselves (and make as much money as they can). They are like people who own funeral parlours who go straight to the newspaper obituaries every day, and if it's nice and thick they're happy.

I believe that from early on Bob led me up the garden path. He told me it was 'all okay' and that 'Everything's being sorted'. Most important, he said I wouldn't go to jail.

Serg and I had separate trials. He went first, and was convicted. And when I was in the dock, the first question my lawyer asked me was: 'Where's your co-accused right now?'

'I beg your pardon?'

'Where's your co-accused right now?'

Of course, I had to answer. 'He's in jail.'

So straightaway it put in the jury's mind that my co-accused was obviously guilty, so I probably was, too. It was a battle from that point on.

When the jury returned with a guilty verdict, I was a little bit shocked. But I still thought it'd be okay and I'd get, maybe, a couple of months. Instead, the judge sentenced me to a year in jail.

I wanted to appeal, but Bob told me not to, because I might get a longer sentence. I couldn't believe it. He'd gone from saying there was no hope in the world I'd go to jail, to me getting a year and him saying, 'Don't appeal; you might get more'!

But in hindsight, the sentence did me a big favour. It not only pulled me up in my tracks—and God knows where I would have finished—but I learned the true value of my family.

The verdict was devastating, though. We had a two-year-old son; Cheryle was heavily pregnant and she had no form of income.

Somehow she managed to keep up the mortgage payments—she even sold her car—and I shall be forever grateful to those friends who helped while I was inside.

The legal fees for the trial had cost tens of thousands of dollars. I had managed to find the money and we mortgaged the house (the lawyers required payment upfront). The trial finished earlier than expected, and I thought I'd get a fair bit of change, probably several thousand dollars, which would help while I was in jail. I told Cheryle to make sure she got the money, and she was onto it.

Shortly before Christmas, Bob called, saying he had the money he owed us—$200. I couldn't believe it when I found out. He lost me that day, but that's the way lawyers are: it's all about the money. Cheryle told him, 'You keep it. You obviously need it more than me'.

I began my sentence at Melbourne's Pentridge Prison in December 1982. It was pretty tough. We used to have to shower in the open and wash our clothes. I saw several people get boiling water thrown over them.

I'd been there only a few days when I saw this bloke walk up and punch another prisoner through the door of his cell. Moments later, the screws came and grabbed me and within days I found myself at a hearing before the governor. They told me an officer had witnessed the attack. I told them it wasn't me, but I wasn't prepared to say who actually did it. (It was a Kiwi bloke who looked a bit like me, except he had a tattoo of a cross on his head.) They gave me a warning: 'If you think you're going to come in here, try to stand over people and be a smarty, well, you'd better think again'. I protested my innocence, but I knew I'd got off on the wrong foot. So I kept my head down.

One thing I hated in jail was the drug use. I'd seen junkies shoot up as a kid, and again I found myself with people hiding in corners and sticking needles in their arms (eight of us were locked up each night in one cell). It made me sick.

On the upside, I met Mario Condello, who became a friend for life. He was intelligent and well educated, but was doing seven years over a number of things—conspiracy to murder, conspiracy to commit arson, drugs. He had a pretty colourful record. He told me about one job in which he bought some prints, insured them as original paintings and put them on a train from Naples to Rome. They blew up the train to claim the insurance, but the train didn't burn properly and they came unstuck. [*Condello was shot dead on 6 February 2006. At the time of writing, no one had been charged with the murder.*]

I worked in the jail kitchen and sometimes managed to pinch a bit of food (meat, pasta and the like) so we could have a cook-up at night. Mario was the chef and he made a pretty good pasta. He also knew an old bloke who worked in the jail's garden, so a few chillies and tomatoes ended up in the pasta, too.

One night, Mario gave me a kiss on the cheek and said, 'Mick, it's nice to have met you'.

'Why?' I asked. 'Are you moving to another jail?'

'No, I'm going tomorrow.'

I thought he was off his head. He was doing seven years. Where was he going?

I found out the next day, when a helicopter tried to land on the jail's tennis court to break out people tied up in a drugs ring—and Mario was going with them. They had a sophisticated getaway plan, and even had plastic surgeons lined up. But the screws started shooting at the helicopter. (They're not allowed to by law because it could endanger the lives of everyone on the ground, but they did it anyway.) In the end, several people were charged over that breakout attempt.

After three months, I was sent to Morwell Prison, in eastern Victoria. It was an 'open prison', which meant the doors weren't locked and you could come out of your cell at any time. We were allowed to go for runs in the nearby mountains. (I got pretty fit, and good at dodging snakes.) I even worked as the jail's barber for a while. We could also make phone calls until late at night, and there were no limits on visitors.

Friends and family, including my mother and father, came every weekend. Most weekends there were twenty or thirty people around a barbecue. They brought a heap of food and, at night, the other inmates used to visit my hut because there was so much food left over. I used to feed half the jail.

Visitors would also leave 'supplies' just outside the prison walls, under a bridge, so we'd get a couple of blokes to run down to it and bring back the Scotch and beer that had been dropped off. That came to a halt towards the end of my spell at Morwell, after a couple of blokes escaped, and they stopped letting us out.

On 22 February 1983, my daughter, Sarah, was born. I had applied to the jail for an eight-hour leave to see Cheryle and the new baby, which at that time was unheard of. No one had been granted such leave before. I had a priest, Father John Brosnan, and some others helping push for me—and it was granted. It was good of them to do it, and I was grateful.

A friend had a very quick car, a Ford GT351, and he picked me up at the prison. We got to Melbourne in about an hour and a half (it normally took two and a half hours) so I could spend as much time as possible with my family. I went straight to the hospital and saw Cheryle and the baby. I was very upset I'd missed the birth, but it was wonderful to be there so soon afterwards. Then I saw my two-year-old son, Damien, who was being looked after by friends.

It broke my heart when it was time to leave; I didn't want to go back. But I knew I had to; otherwise, I'd be charged with escape, and serve more time. So commonsense prevailed. I had about five months left. My friend whizzed me back in his car and we made it in time.

I was released from jail on 26 July 1983. Cheryle came to pick me up, and on the way home we stopped at a big shopping centre. Although I'd been in jail for only eight months, walking though that shopping centre was one of the strangest feelings I've ever had in my life. I felt like I was walking on a different planet, with the noise, the people, the sounds, the lights … Thankfully, it didn't take me long to adjust to life on the outside and I soon developed a routine.

And I knew one thing—I wasn't going back to jail. Ever.

The burglaries and safe-breakings had been an adrenaline rush more than anything else, and I vowed that that part of my life was over. I was a family man with two young children, and I had seen the pain and worry I had put my family through, especially Cheryle. I was determined that it wasn't going to happen again, so I said, 'That's it, no more'—put my cue in the rack. Besides, there were other ways to make money. So I channelled my energies into those.

8

THE TWO-UP

Before being locked up for the golf course burglary, I'd been running a card game in Carlton with several people, including Alphonse Gangitano. When I went inside, I asked my brother, John, to look after my share. It was a disaster. In short, John got into frequent arguments with Alphonse and the other partners. Gamblers, too, were threatened and abused. It became a bloodbath: there was a fight there every night. People stopped going because they were afraid, and we lost a lot of clients. It nearly became very violent and nasty. Thank God it didn't, because someone would have been badly hurt or killed. Alphonse had even come to visit me in jail, telling me how bad things had become. He said he had not 'sorted out' John out of respect for me. So I was pretty anxious to get back to running the business before it was totally destroyed.

Surprisingly, when I was released, the game was still going, which says how strong the business was and how desperate the gamblers were. I started running it by myself and, before long, built it back up again.

THE TWO-UP

At the same time, the Two-Up was having some trouble. I'd sold my share (and started the baccarat game instead) some time before going to jail, and the Two-Up had prospered. But about the time I was on trial, Brian Kane was shot dead. [*He was gunned down in the Quarry Hotel in Brunswick, in November 1982. His niece, Trish, later married Jason Moran, who was himself shot dead in 2003.*] Brian had been 'protecting' the Two-Up for many years and, once he died, they tried to look after themselves. But they couldn't handle it—people were running amok, and there was always trouble. So they paid me to go in and make sure there was no trouble—they paid about $1000 a week, which was pretty good money then.

I did that for about eighteen months, before I heard Nappy Ollington wanted to sell out—it was a great chance to get a decent share. A friend named Les and I jumped at the chance and took a one-third stake (it cost us $80 000). We changed it a lot and turned it into a much bigger business. Innovations included an annual event to raise money for the Royal Children's Hospital. Also, women were allowed in—before then it had been strictly men only. I introduced Christmas parties, where we provided the food and drink. We put on 'special' nights that incorporated different games, such as baccarat, under the one roof.

The Two-Up became an interesting and colourful meeting place, something of a social club, open every day of the year. You couldn't get in unless you were known at the door or you came with someone who was. So it was always an adrenaline rush for some people to be there, the idea of being somewhere illegal. There were many regulars, including a lot of old people. Most days 300 people came through, and there were all types, people from all walks of life. Everyone seemed to have a nickname: Stork, Hand Grenade, Yarra, Bomber. I got to meet lots of people and find out what they did. Some people would come in and sit around, and not even have a bet; they just liked the environment. Things were always being sold, with people saying, 'You want to buy this?' One night a journalist came in with most of the touring English cricket team.

Sometimes we gave credit, but we were careful who we lent money to. No one tells more lies than a gambler—they'll say anything to get a dollar. Often, we lent money and they lost it. We were pretty easy-going: we'd work out terms and get it back. But there were times we had to write the money off. We lost plenty that way over the years. If they didn't have the money, well, you can't get blood out of a stone. But if you knew they had the money and just didn't want to give it back, that was something else. Most of the time when you lent someone big money you'd make sure it was someone reliable, someone who could pay it back. And that included doctors, lawyers, all sorts of professional people. And there were never really any problems.

If someone lost all their money, we'd make sure they got home in a cab, with a bit of money to keep them going. I must have heard every hard-luck story in the world, you know: 'I can't buy groceries this week'. So we used to support most people. We were making a lot of money.

We had at least fifteen people working at each game, and there were three games each day. We employed ex-fighters and blokes that could handle themselves, as long as they had a good outlook on life. We didn't want aggressive people there. We built a very tough, well-respected crew, and they did a good job, treating the customers well to make sure it was a fun atmosphere.

Having a tough crew had its advantages. In the late 1980s, there was a big nightclub in Melbourne's King Street strip that was out of control. One of the owners was using a lot of cocaine and he couldn't handle the club—there was a lot of trouble. So he asked me and a mate to clean it up. For that we got 10 per cent of the business. I opened a section upstairs and called it 'Pensioners' Corner'. All the old blokes went up there, got free drinks and had a great night. Plenty of my friends went. Just our presence there fixed the problem. A lot of the people causing problems knew we were involved, and after only a few weeks the trouble stopped altogether. The owner was pretty pleased, but we weren't earning any profits from our share—the money kept disappearing. It turned out the owner's drug habit was getting worse. We had a couple of arguments and he said he wanted us out. So he paid $60 000 in cash for our 10 per cent and we walked. The free booze was good while it lasted!

In many ways the Two-Up taught me fabulous negotiating skills. I really had to be a psychoanalyst to deal with the different people who came in, from drunks and murderers to businessmen and bank managers. Once, a couple of people tried to start a rival game, and we had to go and give them the bad news. Everyone knew the rules, and if they didn't they were soon told. They shut down pretty quickly. Funnily enough, a couple of them were friends of mine, but they did the right thing. Apart from that, it was all smooth sailing.

When I bought my share, the game was operating under the 'Melbourne way', which meant people bet against each other. Someone might want to bet $1000 on two heads coming up, and various people could bet against him, say in $50 and $100 bets, on the tails. We had benders who kept a very close eye on what was happening. If a customer won three bets in a row, they had to pay a 10 per cent commission on the winnings. (So if they won three bets of $100 each, they paid the house $30.) We used to put that money in a tin and, at the end of the night, we'd add it up. There was always plenty there. Best of all there was no risk—the house couldn't lose.

(Playing the Melbourne way meant there was always cash on the ground as people bet against each other, often thousands of dollars at a time. People used to put chewing gum on the bottom of their shoes, step onto the money then walk off. Most times we caught them, and pulled them up—they'd be warned or thrown out and barred.)

After a while, however, we started playing the 'Sydney way'. This was more lucrative, but it was also risky. Under this method we acted as the bank, and punters bet against the house on one big table. On one side you bet heads, on the other side tails. There used to be about eight of us taking the money at each spin. Winning bets were paid, less a 10 per cent commission. (So a winning $100 bet won $90.) For example, there might be $4000 bet on heads and $500 on tails. If tails came up, the house won $3500 plus commission on the winning tails bids ($50). If heads came up, the house would be down thousands. But on the law of averages the house ended up winning. That's when we started making serious money: $20 000 or $30 000 a week each.

The problem was, I loved to gamble myself. I'd make $20000 one week, and lose $50000 on the weekend. Sometimes I lost it all; other times I was remarkably lucky. One Thursday night, after the Two-Up, I went and played Russian poker at a game in North Melbourne. I took a suitcase with the Two-Up's money—about $70000—and started playing. I lost that, then borrowed from the house. The game had been going about twenty hours—it was now early Saturday morning—and I was down more than $150000. The game was winding up because it was a Saturday morning and the races would soon start. People were leaving.

All of a sudden this Greek property developer called George walked up the stairs. He loved a bet. 'Hello boys', he said. 'What are you playing?'

'Russian poker.'

'How do you play that?'

'Sit down and we'll teach you', I said.

THE TWO-UP

He was there for eight hours and lost $250 000. I paid back the house and recouped my $70 000 plus some extra.

Despite my erratic gambling, I had one priority—to make sure there was enough so all the bills were paid at home. None of my kids went without, including going to good schools. And whatever was left, I used to gamble. Once in a while (and this still happens) I would decide that enough was enough—no more. And I'd start saving, building a nest-egg. At our home in Wheelers Hill I installed a floor safe. I would put my head down and decide not to gamble. Over a period of six months I'd fill the safe—once there was about $400 000 there. Then all of a sudden something would happen, I'd break out gambling, and lose it all. I've done that probably twenty times in my life. Whenever I've had a nest-egg saved—maybe $50 000, $100 000, or a lot more—it's only taken one little outburst of gambling and *bang*, it's all been gone. If I had been half-smart, today I could own half of Lygon Street.

A bloke called Harry used to frequent the Two-Up. Harry was deaf and dumb; in fact, we had a few deaf and dumb blokes come in. When Harry wanted to bet, he held up fingers for the money, and either touched his head (for heads) or his bum (for tails). One day, Harry made a $20 bet on tails against the house, and he won. For a joke, one of the staff who was paying out took Harry's money. So Harry walked up to the table to collect on his winning bet and there was nothing there. He put two fingers up and tapped his bum—$20 on the tail.

And the staff member said, 'No, sorry mate, didn't have the bet on'.

Harry repeated himself, waving two fingers and touching his bum, trying to explain that his bet was there, the money had gone and someone had robbed him.

He was being strung along: 'Can't help you, mate. The money wasn't there …'

This went on for a few minutes, and the whole room was watching, amused, waiting to see what would happen. All of a sudden, Harry turned around and shouted, 'I had fucking $20 on the tail!'

The whole joint erupted, then everyone started clapping, laughing and crying out, 'We've cured him, we've cured him'.

It turned out Harry wasn't actually deaf and dumb; he just didn't want to talk to anyone. He'd been doing it for years.

Another bloke who came frequently to the Two-Up was Chocka, who is a good armed robber, lovely bloke and pretty tough. One day he arrived with a bull terrier and a load of money. He wanted to back the tail, and he bet against everyone (the Melbourne way). There was maybe $10 000 on the throw of the coins, a huge result.

The bloke spinning the coins tossed them in the air. The first came down and was a head; the other was rolling, slowly, and about to roll as a head when Chocka's dog, like it was trained, ran into the ring and grabbed the penny in its mouth. The bender called it a 'no bet'. The coins went up again and fell as two tails. Chocka promptly grabbed all the money and headed straight out the door. That was one well-trained dog.

The Two-Up, of course, was illegal, and attracted plenty of police attention. But the only police who really troubled us were the gaming squad. Their job was to shut us down, and sometimes they raided us two or three times a week. Most other police were happy for us to exist. So we made it as hard as possible for the gaming squad to catch us. We had lookouts in the street, security on the door.

The coppers needed to catch us in the act for charges to stick—they needed the evidence, including the pennies that were spun in the air. So if a police raid started, we'd quickly change the room around and pretend it was a social gathering: we'd sing 'Happy Birthday' or put a video on a big screen. But they knew what was going on. It was a bit of a game.

If they caught us three times they could 'quarantine' the building, meaning it could not be used again for a year for any purpose. So after each successful raid, we moved premises, meaning that over the years the Two-Up had dozens and dozens of homes, often warehouses around the inner city.

One night, the Two-Up was running in Carlton Place, down a skinny laneway. It was dark. A Turkish bloke called Hassan arrived with some mates, and wanted to get in. He was drunk or on drugs, so the doorman refused him entry. Hassan hit the doorman and a big fight started. To cut a long story short, those blokes lost, and left, threatening all sorts of things.

Before long, they came back with a car, drove it down the laneway and ran into the front door, trying to break it open. We were convinced those blokes had guns and had come for revenge. The nit-keeper on the roof was dropping bluestones onto the car, trying to break through the sunroof and hit the driver on the head. (He missed.) It was pretty wild.

They took off, and so did I. My first stop was a phone box—we needed someone down there with a couple of guns in case they came back with guns. I had no idea what those lunatics were doing. I drove back to the Two-Up and saw they were already back in the laneway.

My sister was working upstairs, and there were some old people at the game too. We didn't need madmen with guns in there, so I drove into the lane and shouted at them. It worked. They jumped in their car and started chasing me, and we were flying. They were hanging out their car with something in their hands, and I knew they had guns. This chase went all over Carlton before they stopped on the side of the road near Lygon Street. Hassan opened the bonnet of the car and I thought he was getting out a gun. I don't quite know what happened next, but I lost control of the car and ran into him, squashing him between the two cars. His car ended up 30 metres down the road and he was left on the ground, sitting up, with his legs hanging off.

I jumped out and he looked at me and said, 'That was a good one'.

I thought, 'This bloke's Superman'. I later found out he was on a drug called Rohypnol—they call it the 'Rambo drug' because apparently you don't feel pain.

The next minute, the police arrived and arrested me. I was charged with, among other things, attempted murder.

A few months later, after he got out of hospital, Hassan came to see me. He was on crutches. He told me the police had offered him 24-hour protection, and that they were keen for me to be locked up. And he said, 'If you give me $300 000 I won't give evidence against you'.

'Mate, you do what you have to do', I said. 'You won't be getting anything from me.'

Not long afterwards he was jailed himself—he tried to run a copper over and pulled a gun on him. Hassan was a bit mad. And inside, he died. I've been led to believe he got a 'hot shot', a deliberate overdose where someone stuck a needle in his arm. The police tried to blame me, saying I was behind it. It was absolute rubbish. In the end, the Crown dropped all charges against me.

The police tried every way to catch us at the Two-Up—they put in undercover coppers, climbed through the roof. One night they drilled a hole from the building next door and put a 'snake' through the wall, which had a camera on the end, and they videotaped the whole room while the game was in progress. So when they came in to raid us—by that time we were playing bocce or something—they arrested the lot of us because they had video evidence. They were pretty smart at times.

One bloke who used to play was a welder, and he suggested replacing the front door with an old bank vault door. 'Make it hard for them to get in', he said.

So we did, and, in the end, the police brought their own oxyacetylene cutting equipment, cut the hinges off and took the door away. Each time they did, we got another door and put it up.

One day, the policeman in charge, a superintendent, came to see me. 'Mick, we've got a problem', he said. 'We've got no room left in the yard to put these bloody steel doors.'

'Well, don't take them', I said. 'Leave them there and when you knock we'll let you in.' So we agreed that they wouldn't take any more doors and we would let them in as quickly as we could.

And when the police did come in, I controlled the crowd, saying, 'Now listen, everyone: behave, relax—they're here to do a job. Let them do their job and they're out of here, and we'll start again'.

When I ran the game there was never, ever a problem. Most of the coppers treated me with respect and they got the same in return. (There were a couple of smart, vindictive ones, too, and I told them what I thought of them.) If the coppers took people away to charge them, we'd pay their fine and tell them to hurry back. A lot of square-heads—people who'd never been in trouble with police—loved it. It gave them a sense of excitement. The game usually resumed within an hour or so.

The police could have put us out of business if they had seriously wanted to, but many coppers wanted the game to continue. It was to their advantage to have a place where they could drop in—and they did—and monitor who had money, which was handy after, say, a big armed robbery (there were always a few police informers at the game). Some police would call in and have a look around and we would let the game keep running; there was never a problem. Detectives sometimes came in with interstate police who were visiting Melbourne. They used to have a bet—if they lost their money we'd give it back; if they won they'd walk out with our money. They couldn't lose.

The game was also protected. We paid a monthly sling, which the coppers divided up among themselves. In return we were tipped off when raids were about to take place—I carried a beeper and got messages: 'Be careful: you're going to be raided'. Once we were tipped off about a truckload of police in a van across the road. We ran across and listened in at the van and, sure enough, they were there.

But if there was any major crime in Melbourne, all bets were off. After the Russell Street bombing and the Walsh Street murders, they closed the Two-Up until the cases were solved and they'd found who did them. I never understood the method to their madness. Perhaps they thought they were affecting us and we would divulge who had done it. It had nothing to do with us. I didn't get their mentality. [*In the Russell Street bombing, in 1986, the city's main police station was hit by a car bomb, killing a policewoman and wounding many others. The Walsh Street murders took place in 1988: two uniformed police were shot dead in an ambush.*]

At the time, I was also involved in running a card game upstairs at L'Alba, a Lygon Street restaurant. The games were sometimes huge, and there was excellent food provided. Police often dropped in for a steak and a beer (at no cost). They'd watch the game from a distance, and wouldn't interfere. It was a good arrangement.

One night I was quite drunk, driving Graham Kinniburgh home, when I was pulled over by the police in Kew. I blew into a breathalyser. The copper looked at the result, looked at me, and said, 'Mate, you're blind'.

I looked at him. 'Mate, I feed half the police force.'

'What do you mean?'

'I run L'Alba in Lygon Street. Half of you blokes come in for a feed.' I kept going. 'Come up there sometime; you'd be welcome as my guest.'

'All right, we will', said the copper. 'Drive carefully.'

'Yeah, I will.'

I was pretty lucky that night, especially as I preach to my kids not to drink and drive! I feel like the pot calling the kettle black.

Because I used to handle big money (often a bank of $60000 or more in cash), I often carried a gun. I knew I was a target. I also had a high profile (although not as high as today), which meant people wanted to have a crack at me. So I was careful with my routine. I never flaunted the fact I was carrying a gun; in fact, most people wouldn't have had any idea. Carrying a gun was, simply, a necessary evil. Luckily, I never needed to use it.

I wasn't the only one carrying a gun. One night at a card game in North Melbourne, for a joke, the dealer (whose name was Bodgie) pulled a knife and put it on the table. It was a full table, about a dozen blokes.

And someone else, for a joke, said, 'Limit, raise' [*as if increasing the bet*], pulled out a gun and put it on the table in front of him.

The next bloke pulled out his gun and said, 'More limit'.

And within a few moments there were about eight guns on the table. It was very funny.

In the late 1980s, Chopper Read was released from jail. Chopper was at war with Alphonse Gangitano, and there were rumours he wanted to get me, too. (I thought I was involved at the time, but it turned out Chopper didn't have a problem with me.) Chopper was running around Melbourne, armed, and wearing a neck-to-waist bullet-proof vest.

I contacted Lewis Moran and bought a gun to protect myself—an Armalite pistol, with ammunition that pierced steel. 'That should deal with Chopper's bullet-proof vest', I thought.

I never went looking for Chopper, but if he came near me and wanted to have a crack, I knew I'd have a chance. I carried this gun for quite a few months, until Chopper was locked up again, after killing a bloke outside Bojangles Nightclub. [*Read was charged with murder and was remanded in custody. When his case came to trial, he argued that he had acted in self-defence. He was found not guilty by the jury.*]

With Chopper out of the way, I had no more need for the gun, so I sold it to a mate. A week later, he came back to me and said, 'The gun's no good'.

I asked him what he meant.

'It hasn't got a firing pin. It doesn't work.'

And he was right. It didn't. I'd been running around with a loaded Armalite pistol thinking I had some sort of chance. I learned a golden rule that day: if you ever buy a gun, make sure it works.

One night I went for a drink with a friend, Noel, at a club called the Crest. It was meant to be a quiet drink, but we came across this team of blokes from Sydney who were being really smart. There were six or eight of them. Anyway, one thing led to another, and a fight started. We were in the right—we didn't do anything wrong. I was pretty fit and strong, and so was Noel, and we gave it to them and left bodies lying everywhere. And that was that.

A few nights later, Yugoslav Tony, one of the bouncers at the Crest, who also worked on the door at the Two-Up, came in and grabbed me. 'Mick, a team of blokes have come from Sydney. They're looking for you over that blue, and they want to kill you.'

We made some inquiries and found that they were supposedly a well-known crew. They'd headed to a massage parlour in Footscray. So I decided we should take the initiative and pay them a visit. I grabbed three or four blokes. I said, 'Let's go and see them; we'll sort it out'.

I was about to jump in my car when a good friend, Georgie, said, 'Don't get in your car; jump in my car. It's not even registered to me'.

For good measure, Georgie had a shotgun in the boot. Not that it mattered—we were all loaded anyway.

We drove down to the parlour and burst in, and the Sydney crew was there. 'Looking for us, were you?' I asked. Guns drawn, we simply terrorised those blokes. They were crying and carrying on like babies. It was embarrassing. But we wanted it known that if they were looking to do us harm, we were prepared—and this was what we were prepared to do. In the end they apologised profusely, and that was the end of it. We didn't hear from them again.

Alphonse Gangitano often came to the Two-Up, and from time to time he'd play up. He hated losing. Sometimes he was just a little bit annoyed when he lost; other times he'd scream, yell and carry on. Sometimes he threatened people.

One night he went to throw the pennies into the air and a gun fell out the back of his pants. He was standing in front of 200 people. The police knew within about eight minutes (there were plenty of police informers there) and we got raided.

We had a few discussions afterwards about what to do, and decided Alphonse had to be barred. I was designated to tell him, because he respected me—and he probably would have battered anyone else. So I went to see him and told him he was barred.

'Mate, you can't do that.'

'We've got to', I told him. 'This is our bread and butter. We all live off this joint, and you're ruining it for us. The police are getting involved now. So that's it.'

He was upset and we didn't talk for a while. Later, we became friends again. He understood in the end that business is bigger than any one person.

THE TWO-UP

In about 1987, Alphonse Gangitano set up his own [*illegal*] casino at a club in Nicholson Street, in Fitzroy. They were beautiful premises; he and a few others had pumped a fair bit of money into it. At the time, I wasn't talking to Alphonse because we'd fallen out. I distinctly remember the night his casino opened, because there was next to no one at the Two-Up. The big gamblers were all at Alphonse's new place. Even worse, a couple had dropped in and we were down $12 000—they'd won the money off us and promptly left for the new casino.

We were sitting there, brooding, when a champion trotting driver named Vinnie called in. 'G'day', he said. 'The new casino that's opened—do you know where it is?'

'Mate, that's in Frankston.' [*An hour's drive away—in reality, the casino was just around the corner.*]

'You're joking', he said. 'I'm not going all the way down there.'

So Vinnie came in and started playing two-up—he had about $4000 cash with him. In a short time he lost that, then did a stack on credit, about $80 000 (he was good for it, and paid up). His main problem was that he was betting tails, and Yugoslav Tony, one of the blokes who worked at the Two-Up, spun an incredible thirteen heads in a row. We ended up winning the bulk of Vinnie's money, $50 000 or $60 000, with the other players who'd come in that night winning about another $20 000.

The best part, though, came a couple of months later, when I started talking to Alphonse again. He told me that on the night of the opening, Vinnie had turned up and Alphonse had welcomed him, knowing he was a big punter.

'I just done $80 000 at the Two-Up', was Vinnie's opening line.

Alphonse couldn't believe it. In the end, the casino only lasted a couple of weeks because the police hated Alphonse and they closed it down.

Eventually, however, I got out of the Two-Up, selling my share in about 1989 to a bloke called Geoff. I'd had enough, especially with my partners. There was conflict, and I decided to get out and do my own thing. The Two-Up had been an amazing business and I'd been lucky to be a part of it. Those who took over didn't run it too professionally, but they still got people there. It was incredible: it didn't matter what they did; the gamblers just kept going back.

But once Melbourne's Crown Casino opened, in 1994, the Two-Up was finished. It was threatening government revenue—like SP bookmakers did when the Totaliser Agency Board (TAB) opened years earlier—so the authorities moved hard to shut it down. The fines went from $10 per head and $100 for running the game to $100 a head and $1000 for running it. Then it became $1000 a head, enough to scare away the punters. For those running the game, 200 people in a room could cost you $200 000. The doors were shut, and the Two-Up was over.

9

PLAYING GAMES

Over the years, I ran a series of illegal gaming operations: blackjack, dice-in-a-cage, baccarat, Russian poker, SP bookmaking and more. Games would open and close, depending on money, police raids and different partnerships. I made millions—and gambled away just as much.

At many games, such as two-up and baccarat, the house took 10 per cent of winning bets. In the card game manilla, the house typically took 5 per cent of the pot. Some of these games were massive, and huge earners for the house. Yet the most profitable business I ever ran was an SP bookmaking operation that I established after leaving the Two-Up.

There were already lots of SP bookies around Melbourne, but I'd learned from Bruce Johnstone that there were some big punters who scared most bookies, such as George Freeman [*a 'colourful racing identity' from Sydney, who died in 1990*]. Sometimes these big punters won, but nine times out of ten they lost. When a huge bet was made, bookmakers would be ringing each other trying to lay off [*bet with other bookmakers*], because they didn't want to hold all the money and face a massive payout if the horse won. So I ran around all these SP bookmakers and told them, 'Whatever you want to back, you can back with me. And I don't care how much'. The next minute these big, big bets started coming in. I was flooded.

I set up in Melbourne's Hilton Hotel, the Southern Cross Hotel and other places, with four or five phones. It didn't take long to build a good clientele base. I even picked up some Arab sheikhs who would bet up to $20000 on every favourite, in every race, in every state. It was a goldmine.

I've been on both ends of betting: where I've owed and where I've been owed. There's plenty of history at both ends of the scale. Some weeks I was making $300000 or $400000. But when a heavily backed horse won, it cost a fair bit of money. A couple of times I couldn't cover the debts, but I managed to get through, and one way or another they were always paid. I remember one bloke: I owed him $90000, and I couldn't pay. I said, 'Do me a favour—I'll sort it out next week'.

He said, 'No problems'.

And the next day he rang up, had a bet—because punters can't help themselves—and lost back the $90 000 plus some more.

Sometimes people didn't pay up. If they didn't have the money, I just used to accept it. It was my fault for taking the bet. You can't get blood out of a stone. But if people had the money and didn't want to pay, it was a different story. I could get nasty and I made sure I got it. I didn't belt people or threaten to take them away in the boot of a car. Instead, we'd sit down and mediate: 'We're not here to harm you; we want to know exactly where you stand. We want to resolve this issue'. We'd try to settle it amicably.

The only time I got myself into trouble was when I bet myself. Unfortunately, being a mad punter, as quickly as I made money I'd throw it away. In the end it destroyed the SP goldmine I'd established, which could have set me up financially for life. And sometimes my gambling got a bit silly. Once I was losing $1 million with a bloke in Sydney, and he really put the screws on me: he wouldn't let me on [*bet any more*]. 'You can only get on for $20 000', he said.

'But I'm losing a million.'

'I don't care', he said. 'That's all you're getting on for.'

I remember ringing up and saying, 'I want $300 000 on this horse'—it was a favourite in Adelaide.

'No, you can't get on.'

So, just before the race, I rang his office and said, 'It's Mick from Melbourne. I want $300 000 on the horse to win'. And I hung up the phone. It was just desperation. I didn't have $1 million to pay him.

The horse won, and I ended up being owed $1.3 million back. And this bookie rang me and said, 'You weren't on it; I never accepted the bet'.

'Yes you did', I said. My argument was that he didn't say I *wasn't* on. I was in the wrong, but desperate times call for desperate acts.

'You're not on and you're not getting paid', he said.

And I said, 'Stick it up your arse. We're square'.

Not long afterwards, this bloke actually approached a couple of friends of mine in Tasmania and said, 'There's $20 000 if you go and break his arms and legs'.

They rang me and told me.

So I phoned the bookmaker. 'Mate, I hear you're shopping around trying to get my arms and legs broken', I said. 'If I hear it again, I'm going to jump on a plane, come up there and break your arms and legs. You understand?'

And he said, 'Yes, I understand'.

When I couldn't pay, I was just stupid. It was probably lucky I didn't get hurt or killed. It's funny, because I'd seen people destroy themselves, lose their money and lose their lives, so I knew better than anyone that you couldn't win. But when it's in your blood, it's difficult to stay away.

In the early 1990s, I put some money into a bonbonnière business. (When Europeans get married, at the end of the night when the people leave there are bonbonnières on the table—a gift for everyone. It might be a candle-holder or a toothpick-holder or something made of crystal—plus three or four almonds covered with icing.) It was a pretty good business. I had two partners, both Italian blokes, and we all borrowed money to buy it. What I didn't know was that one of my partners was very close to the bank manager who lent us the money—and that when I signed a loan for $200 000, I unknowingly signed papers that gave a running mortgage on my house.

One of the partners, Mario [*not Mario Condello*], started new businesses using the cash, and I failed to monitor it. I was pretty young and green, and I went with the flow. And while the bonbonnière business was doing okay, everything else went bad and the whole venture went belly-up. (Mario became known as The Bird Man after being caught smuggling birds—last time I heard of him he was in jail.) They lost about $200000 each, but I lost my house, which was worth about $1 million (although the bank sold it for $350000 in a depressed market). It was a beautiful property, on an acre, with a pool and tennis court. We used to get all sorts of wildlife: snakes, kangaroos, koalas. The house was magnificent, Mediterranean-style with five bedrooms and a big entertaining area. It was my dream home at the time.

PLAYING GAMES

I went to the Supreme Court to fight to keep my house—we thought we had a good case—but we lost. And then the tax man said he wanted $300 000 for undeclared income. By this point I was broke, and had no house. Either they were going to bankrupt me or I was going to bankrupt myself. So I did it voluntarily in March 1993.

Some months later, I borrowed $50 000 from a friend, and we put a deposit on a house in Doncaster. I put it in the kids' names so it could never be taken away again.

My father was a hard-working man all his life. In his late seventies, though, he developed pretty bad cataracts in his eyes and began driving through red lights. He had to give work away. Instead, he stayed home—and he hated it. In the end, he had a massive stroke. The doctor who assessed him told me, 'Mick, it's a very, very severe stroke, probably one of the worst we've seen for a long time. We don't think he will survive twenty-four hours'.

Dad survived three and a half years.

He was completely paralysed down one side, and couldn't talk or walk. He sat there and acknowledged me by nodding his head. At first he just wanted to die. They put drips in him because he wouldn't eat, and he would pull them out. We had to tie his arm down to the bed so they could feed him intravenously.

After a few months he relaxed a bit, and we started feeding him ourselves. We had him in a nursing home because he couldn't be looked after at home, and I used to see him just about every day. On weekends I would go and grab him—I'd lift him up and put him in the car, put the wheelchair in the boot and take him home.

The first couple of times when we left to take him back to the nursing home, he grabbed the walls at the side of the door. He didn't want to go. It broke my heart; he had to go back. My mother just couldn't look after him at home.

We took him out of the nursing home to celebrate his eightieth birthday. It was a lovely day for him; there was forty or fifty of us at a restaurant and he enjoyed it. But it was sad to see him in that state.

One morning, as I was driving my son Damien to school, the phone rang. It was the hospital. A doctor said, 'He wants to go; he is really frail and weak. We can give him morphine to keep him going. We will probably be able to keep him alive for another week or two. But our advice is that you let him go, let him go peacefully'.

I told the doctor, 'Okay, if you think that's what we should do, just let him go peacefully'.

As I said this, tears streamed out of my eyes. My son turned around, looked at me and started crying himself. And he often says, 'Dad, I've only ever seen you cry once in your life', and he reflects on that quite a bit.

My father died on 17 May 1992. I often go to his grave and pay my respects.

I've never been a big racing fan, but in the early 1990s I bought into a couple of trotting horses—Uncle Sessell, who we paid nothing for, and who won about ten races, and Revitalise, who came from New Zealand and cost a fair bit, about $20 000. I enjoyed watching the horses at the track. Revitalise was brilliant in his first race, but suffered a hairline crack in his leg. No one realised and we kept racing him, wondering why he didn't win again.

One day they were both set to race at a country meeting. A few of us went, and we left first thing because one horse was in an early race. And as we were driving up the highway, we saw a horse float broken down on the side of the road. It was my horse trainer, Max, with Uncle Sessel and Revitalise.

I pulled over and got out. 'Max, what's happened? What's wrong?'

'I've snapped an axle on the car', he said.

I used to drive a big Ford LTD (the long one that looked like an aeroplane). It had a towbar on the back. 'I'll tow it', I said.

Max looked at his watch. 'We have to have them there half an hour before the first race; otherwise, they scratch them.'

'Okay', I said. 'No worries.'

Max managed to get a lift with someone else (my car was full). We hitched up the float and I set off. I'd never towed much before, except for a trailer of rubbish to the tip. Anyway, I put my foot down—it was a powerful car—and soon forgot I was towing the two horses. But not for long. As I went into a corner the whole car lifted up, the float lifted up, and we nearly rolled. This happened a few times, and once or twice I was convinced we were going over.

When we came to traffic lights in a town, I braked—and not much happened. The weight of the horse float pushed us through the red light and into the intersection. I was lucky there was nothing in front of us; we would have ploughed into it. I didn't realise you had to brake early because of the extra weight.

We got to the race track on time. Max unhooked the float, opened the back doors and looked in. 'What have you done?' he said.

Both horses were on the ground, spread-eagled in a starfish position. It was the funniest thing you've ever seen in your life.

'Mate, I had to get here in a hurry', I said. 'So we went round corners a bit quickly.'

Max kept staring at the horses. 'What have you done to them? I can't believe it.'

Anyway, he tried to get them out of the float, but they wouldn't move. They wouldn't stand up. In the end, it took a couple of people to drag them out.

Max came up to me. 'I really don't believe they're a betting proposition', he said. 'I think they might have run their race.'

'No, they'll be okay', I said. They were in good form and I was still pretty confident they had a winning chance. I backed both of them—and they both ran last. We had a few more bets, then drove home.

That night, Max phoned me. 'Mick, you've ruined these horses', he said.

'Why? What do you mean?'

'I tried to get them into the float, and they were rearing, bucking and jumping, God knows what. I got some help and we finally got them in—and they went straight into the starfish position on the ground.'

I couldn't stop laughing. But from that day on, whenever those horses went into a float, they went straight to the ground in the starfish position. It was the end of their racing careers, so I ended up giving them away to a couple of kids, who loved them and looked after them.

A constant in Lygon Street's gambling scene is a bloke called Genaro, a nice bloke but a mad punter. One day, Genaro put a fortune on a greyhound at Sandown. This dog was all but guaranteed to win if it jumped first and got to the front. Genaro knew it needed to jump first and, to hedge his bets, he went to the starting position, drilled a hole in the fence and looked through, waiting for the race to start.

The dogs jumped—and his dog wasn't first. Genaro knew it couldn't win and he'd come prepared. He threw a live rabbit over the fence into the path of the greyhounds, and caused mayhem, as the dogs started chasing the real rabbit. It was declared a 'no race' and Genaro got his money back.

In about 1992, I talked Mario Condello into putting about $200000 into a new SP bookmaking operation. 'I think we can turn it into a lot of money', I told him. And I was right.

We used a coffee lounge in Queensberry Street, North Melbourne, where the gamblers could play cards, and watch the races on Sky TV. Gamblers could place their bets there—handing over the cash—or ring the bets through to us. Big punters and SP bookmakers would call us directly. We worked at a different address, out of Mario's office in Nicholson Street, Fitzroy, where he did property conveyancing during the week. It was pretty secure, with a huge front window and a door with steel bars.

Every week we were winning $50000, $80000, $150000—it went so well that we started looking at buying property. (I wasn't that interested, but Mario was pretty ambitious.) So, one Saturday, Mario and I went to an auction. We missed out on the house because it went for more than we were prepared to pay. Unbeknown to me, there were two or three gaming squad police watching us.

We got back to Mario's office and started business—Saturday was a big day with the afternoon races. Ron Bongetti was taking bets, and a bloke called Dominic, from Adelaide, had dropped by, to tell us about someone who had died and their funeral arrangements.

All of a sudden the front window caved in. Everyone froze—they weren't used to this—but I knew it was the police.

There was a heap of bets on the table, written on special dissolving paper in case of a police raid. I grabbed them and ran to the back of the office, throwing them into the toilet. That got rid of the evidence. Meanwhile, the police had barged in. The poor bloke from Adelaide was smashed to the ground. Mario was on the floor too. I could hear him yelling and screaming. And then four coppers ran down the hallway to where I was. I thought they'd try to grab me, so I went mental, shouting at them.

'Relax, Mick', they said. 'Sit down, mate, there's no problem.' They were a bit wary of me.

Then the phone started ringing. We had a codeword for placing bets—something like 'Star Trek' (it changed regularly). If we didn't say the particular word, you couldn't bet. The police answered the phones. And these imbecile punters—because they are mad and just want to get the bet on—began giving police all their bets, even though they hadn't been given the codeword: $20000 on this and $15000 on that. And so the police had us cold.

Ronnie, though, had a bad turn. The coppers had run in with guns drawn, and put one to his head. I thought maybe he'd panicked, but he was a tough old bugger, so that didn't make sense. They raced him to hospital, and it turned out he had fluid building up in his body and was slowly drowning. It was a bit touch and go for a while, and he was lucky to pull through. If the police hadn't raided us when they did, Ronnie probably would have died.

The police also raided my home. Cheryle said she saw some police running up the driveway with sledgehammers. She opened the door so they didn't break it down.

We kept the business going after that raid, but everything we touched went bad. We'd saved several hundred thousand dollars— enough to buy a property—but we just lost it all back. So we gave the SP away.

When we finally got to court we started bargaining with the prosecution. We asked if one of us pleaded guilty, could the other two get off? They agreed. So Mario said he would plead guilty. They said no. Ronnie offered to plead guilty. They said no. So, in August 1993, I ended up nodding my head to it. I was fined $20 000.

After the SP folded, I opened a baccarat game off Lygon Street with Mario Condello and a friend called Michael, a regular businessman who'd never been on the wrong side of the law in his life. It was a huge eye-opener for him, an introduction to a new world. As my lawyer Robert Richter told the jury in my 2005 murder trial, 'There's a different world out there you don't know about. There's a different world'. [*Michael has since said, 'I'd never seen anything like it; it was all new to me. I'd usually be in bed by 11 p.m., but that was when we started work—11 p.m. I thought everybody went to bed by midnight or 1 a.m., but that's when "the underworld" came out. The games would go to 6 a.m. or 7 a.m., sometimes later. It was a different life, different world, different people. Before we started, Mick said, "Look, I just want to tell you now what could happen: any night, the police could knock the doors down, run in with guns and point a shotgun at your head". I thought, "What am I getting myself into here?" But it never happened. We only ever had one baccarat table in this place down Argyle Lane.*

There were three or four other tables. People would come, sit down, have coffees and play their own card games—we had nothing really to do with them; we just had our one table. We paid for the coffees—the bill was about $700 a week—and provided soft drink and food. We paid the rent, and staff cost about $6000 a week—a bloke on the door, a bloke in the street, a couple of others and ourselves. The game ran for about eleven months, until the casino opened. It was never raided. I reckon between the three of us, for the time we were in, we made $1 million profit. And that was only one table. It just goes to show the sort of profit that they can make at the casino'.]

10

CROWN CASINO

In 1994, Crown Casino brought about the end of illegal gambling in Victoria. Overnight, the gaming clubs in Chinatown shut down, as did the Two-Up and almost every illegal casino. In many ways I was lost. I didn't know what to do. I had never learned a trade; I had no expertise in any area. Gambling was all I knew—running clubs and running games. I was bankrupt, and we'd lost our dream home. So, in the first couple of years, I spent a lot of time gambling at the casino, trying to make a living. It was pretty hard.

It wasn't long before I found myself in the Mahogany Room, which is set aside for high-rollers, where I knew a lot of the gamblers. Soon I was going there most days, often with Ron Bongetti. We felt quite comfortable there, and I started gambling. There was no natural light, and sometimes I was there for two or three days. Overall, I lost money. The house always wins. But when I gamble, I find some of the money just sticks to my hands.

We were spoiled when it first opened: everything was paid for by the casino—food, drinks, cigars, cigarettes. They trimmed it all down after a while when they realised that too much money was going out the door—people were taking four or five packets of cigarettes, cigars and God knows what.

I used to play baccarat and some of the other games—and I loved the pokies. I knew you couldn't win on them, but I found them relaxing. Over the years I did have some big wins: one weekend I won $300000 on two particular machines. I went back on the Monday to play them again and they were gone. I think they took them away to put them under a microscope and see if I'd done something to them. But I hadn't.

Once I was playing blackjack when the dealer dealt me two aces. I split the aces and she gave an eight and a nine. So I was on nineteen and twenty. The next minute she pulled about seven cards and made twenty-one. I couldn't believe it. In exasperation I threw my arms up—and flicked an ashtray, which flew through the air, ash everywhere. Moments later, out of the corner of my eye, I saw these security blokes running towards us. I thought, 'They're going to have a crack at me'. I spun around, ready—they were armed with little vacuum cleaners, and they hoovered up all the ash.

I was well known at the casino. If there was any trouble, someone playing up badly, they'd often come to me. 'Mick, do you know these people?' I'd say 'yes' or 'no'—they'd always consult me. I'd get calls in the Mahogany Room from security wanting to know about people, including those who said they knew me. There was plenty of respect there.

In the Mahogany Room, millions of dollars changed hands. And baccarat was the game of choice. One night, Mario Condello was sitting at the same table as Tony Santic, whose horse Makybe Diva won three successive Melbourne Cups. Santic was betting $50000 or $100000 a shot. Mario was playing $5000 or $10000.

Mario asked me if I wanted to play, if I needed some money. I said 'no'. Then I said 'yes'. (I was broke.) Mario opened his jacket and pulled out an old, smelly sock full of $5000 chips. He pulled out one chip, gave it to me, then put the sock away. I lost. I borrowed a further $10000. I lost. Mario kept pulling out this sock and giving me more chips. Before long I was down about $90000, which was all his money. Mario wasn't too happy.

Anyway, I left and went and found another $5000 and came back, and this time played on my own. I won four bets, and kept doubling up. A crowd had gathered and each time I won, they clapped. The pile of chips grew bigger.

I had $80000 on the table, on the banker. The dealer was set to deal when, for a joke, I took my shoe off and put it to my ear. 'Yes, Kerry', I said loudly. 'It's going to be a player now, is it? Oh, thanks a lot, Kerry.' [Kerry Packer was the casino's owner.]

I put my shoe back on, moved all the chips from the banker to the player, and waited for the dealer. The next result was the player, so I won. I was, literally, laughing. I gave Mario back his $90000 and put the other $70000 into my pocket.

Mario spent a lot of time at the casino, and he devised a 'foolproof' method of winning on the roulette wheel. It was a simple system: he would leave out seven numbers—the bottom three: 34, 35, 36; the top three: 1, 2, 3; and the 0. All the other numbers he'd put money on.

You could track the most recent fourteen numbers that had won on the display at the roulette tables, and Mario's trick was to go to a table where the bottom seven numbers had come out three times in the fourteen spins. The odds were that those numbers wouldn't come up again. The idea was to have one spin, collect your winnings and go. If you lost, you had five more spins to get your money back, then one more spin.

Mario started by betting $50 a number, an outlay of $1500. He'd have the one spin, and win $1800—a $300 profit. Mario was doing this every day for a long time before I found out about it. When I did, he got annoyed, and even asked for commission. I began betting with Michael (I knew he wouldn't spend the bank) and we were soon winning $300 a day—and then Mario increased his bet to $100 a number, which was $3000 on the table to win $600. Then we increased our bet to $6000 ($200 a number) to win $1200. And Mario started betting $12 000 a spin to win $2400.

Before long, Michael and I had amassed almost $40 000. Mario was going a couple of times a day and was up about $160 000. One night we were chatting with a bloke called Howard, who was running the casino. He had seen what was going on and said, 'You know, boys, you're going to come unstuck with that system'. And, sure enough, one morning Mario went in for his usual bet, and lost. He followed the system and had another go. In a very short time he lost the whole $160 000. Michael went down with our money the same morning, and didn't see Mario or know he'd lost all his money. And the same thing happened. We lost our $40 000.

What Howard had been telling us was that the casino could train a croupier to spin in a small section of the wheel—within three or four numbers. And our seven numbers were in the one place on the wheel. (If you see a heap of money on the table and one or two numbers have nothing on them, that's where the croupier will try to land it, especially in the high-roller rooms where the bets are huge.) They knew we were playing that way, and they found an expert croupier to spin the wheel. Easy come, easy go.

11

THE UNION BUSINESS

I've always had a wide network of friends and associates—from police and businessmen to bank managers and lawyers. And along the way I met a few people from the trade union movement. One day in about 1995, a union official asked if I could do him a favour. The union was having a problem at a dispute in North Melbourne where the workers had set up a picket line outside a factory. The dispute was about the use of non-union labour on the site. Members of the union hierarchy had been on the picket line and had seen a notorious ex-policeman, Brian Murphy, drive past. Murphy was looking at them, watching them—and they were intimidated. Worse, they thought Murphy's front-seat passenger was Tom Domican. They were worried something bad was going to happen. [*Domican was a colourful and feared figure from Sydney who was tied up in Labor Party politics and the building industry.*]

Murphy had had a big reputation around town as a fearless copper who got things done. When I was young and was caught stealing in a South Melbourne bike shop, he was already known as a tough copper—and he gave me a hiding then. He'd since left the police force and set himself up as a consultant.

I knew Murphy and got along well with him, so when John Setka, an organiser with the Construction, Forestry, Mining and Energy Union (CFMEU), asked if I could help, I was happy to see what I could do. I met Murphy for a coffee and we had a chat. He told me Domican hadn't been his passenger—it was a lawyer—but conceded he was there himself to intimidate the union and break up the picket line. There could well have been another step taken if I hadn't become involved. Murphy said he was happy to step back and let it go, a move I really appreciated. 'I won't interfere; but use it to your advantage', he said. 'This means they owe you a favour.'

I went back to John and told him I'd sorted out the matter and he had no further worries. John was grateful, and from that moment word spread about my ability to solve problems. More importantly, I gained some acceptance and credibility among the union people, which developed into a good working relationship.

John, who is an excellent union leader and a great bloke, introduced me to some different people, and via those introductions I met a range of union leaders, including the state secretary of the CFMEU Martin Kingham, assistant state secretary Bill Oliver, vice-president Matt Hudson, John Van Camp, the Victorian secretary of FEDFA, the crane union, and Tony Murphy and Earl Setches from the plumbers' union. Before long I started working for builders and developers, helping to sort out their union problems. I ended up with a pretty good clientele and, for making their problems go away, I was reimbursed quite handsomely.

Many times, I've explained how I make my money from building negotiations—to a royal commission, a court, the taxman and others—but few people seem to get it. They say, 'You're getting paid for nothing'. I don't get paid for nothing. Put simply, the unions can be very militant in Victoria. They can go onto a building site and shut it down for any reason—perhaps the shed where they eat lunch has no air-conditioning, or there are exposed electrical cords (which could be quite dangerous). They just close the joint down. A lot of builders and developers have no relationship with the unions. If the unions get aggressive, the builders are intimidated. So I go in and act as a buffer—no one yells and screams at me—and I get results.

Each time I sign on a new builder or developer, I ring the union and tell them 'He's with me', and that if there are any problems they should call me. Then if something comes up, the union gets in touch: 'Mick, there's a problem. We need to fix it; otherwise, we have to stop the job'. Most times it's easy to fix, but, most importantly for the builders, there's no productivity loss. The job never stops. They love it. And the builders under my 'umbrella' get looked after that way. Without me there, the union would just stop the job and send the workers home; the builders could lose a fortune.

I've learned, however, that some disputes can't be fixed, such as when a new builder takes over a job and money is owed to sub-contractors. The union won't move on that; the outstanding money has to be paid. And there's no way around health and safety issues. But providing you do the right thing, there's never a problem. In my experience, 90 per cent of issues can be resolved.

I owe much of my negotiating skills to the Two-Up, where I was involved in some way for twenty years. Dealing with all sorts of people sharpened my skills at resolving conflict, settling issues and making sure there was no trouble. I've done mediating all my life, and have managed to get work that way.

When I started, I was paid by various builders perhaps $1000 or $2000 a week. Some weeks I was making $10000. One builder was paying me $10000 a month and, when I went to jail in 2004, he said to my family, 'Even if Mick does twenty years' jail, I'll still pay him'. That was how happy this bloke was with the service.

To this day I still work for developers and builders, negotiating deals and agreements with unions. And I still have good friends in the unions—they are pretty fair with me, and we have a good working relationship.

One morning in about 2001, a group of police and investigators came to my house in Doncaster. They were from the royal commission investigating the building industry, and they had a search warrant. [*The royal commission, headed by the Honourable Terence Cole, QC, was set up in August 2001, and its final reports were tabled in the Federal Parliament in March 2003. Its terms of reference included inquiring into inappropriate or unlawful industrial practices such as fraud, collusion, violence and inappropriate payments.*]

'Do me a favour', I asked them. 'Let my family have a shower, have breakfast and go to work—then come in and do what you like.' And they agreed.

An hour or so later they came inside. They spent hours there, and took just about everything they could lay their hands on—personal photos, letters, papers. They carted boxes of stuff away. (About a year later most of it came back, after I made a formal request.) It turned out they were looking at the union deals struck at the redevelopment of the National Gallery of Victoria, deals I had been closely involved with. Funnily enough, I did the negotiations as a favour for a friend and I didn't earn a cent from them. It came back to bite me, though, costing a small fortune in legal bills and exposing me to plenty of unwanted publicity.

For years, I'd largely stayed out of the media spotlight. In the 1980s, Derryn Hinch had run a television story about me and the Two-Up. And I'd been mentioned in a newspaper story in 1998 linking me to the murder of Joe Arena. (It was rubbish, and embarrassing—I know the Arena family well.) But those were nothing compared with what happened in early 2002, when I appeared at hearings of the royal commission, and found myself on television and in all the papers. It was pretty full-on. I didn't like the attention for one minute, but there was nothing I could do about it. I had to cop it on the chin. The publicity concerned quite a few of the builders I worked for, especially the bigger companies, because their names were thrown up in relation to me. But it didn't stop any of them from being my clients. They kept paying me.

I was called to give evidence with a good friend, Dave Hedgcock. I've known Dave for thirty-five years, since we trained together at Kevin Watterson's gym. He has always worked in security, and these days he runs a pretty big outfit that does a lot of security work across Australia.

If anyone was ever going to die of lead poisoning, it'd be Dave. He's been shot three or four times, and that's why we call him 'The Rock'. The last time he was shot was with a .45, a large-calibre gun. Someone climbed over his back fence and, as he came to the door, they shot him. They fired a few shots, but only one hit him—it went right through his pelvis. He crawled back into the house and called a friend. And ten days later, he was refereeing a fight—I couldn't believe it. I grabbed him after the fight and said, 'Mate, you're off your head; you've just been shot'. There was blood seeping out of the wound.

'I can't show any weakness', he replied.

Crazy. But he's a good bloke.

The case revolved around a mate of Dave's called Peter Barker, who worked for a large electrical company that was having trouble getting an agreement signed with the union on the National Gallery site in Melbourne. So Dave had approached me—he knew that I had union contacts—and asked if I could help. Over a few weeks I'd had a series of meetings and, in the end, a deal was put together.

A key part of the problem had centred on a union bloke that the builders didn't want to employ. They'd had bad experiences with him in the past and simply didn't want him there. But in the end they had to take him, and I had secured a guarantee from this bloke that he wouldn't cause any trouble. And things went smoothly and there was never a problem. I delivered, and everyone had been happy.

The successful deal had involved a payment of $275000 to Barker, with some money going to Dave. I got nothing, as it was a favour for Dave. The bloke who paid was sacked by his company. He gave evidence during that royal commission that the reason he had paid the money was that he had been frightened—that people associated with the deal had been known to 'break legs'. But that wasn't the truth—the truth was he had paid it happily.

It was an absolute storm in a teacup. In the end, nothing came of it. There were no charges. (The case did attract the attention of the taxman, who made further extensive inquiries in 2003 that ended with a big settlement in 2005—more on that later.) There was a huge number of people working on the commission, which went on for months. For the lawyers, police and investigators, it was a great way to earn a big living, and I told them that when they questioned me. They didn't like that, but it was the truth. All royal commissions end up achieving nothing, except costing the taxpayers countless millions, this one included. [*In his final report, the royal commissioner concluded, in part, that the National Gallery case 'illustrates graphically* *the problems within the building and construction industry in Victoria (and) ... the central role and the immense power wielded by the building unions'. The royal commissioner was on an annual salary of $660 000, according to one newspaper report.]*

12

ALPHONSE

When I first met Alphonse Gangitano, he was a really good bloke. I knew him as a kid growing up, and he was a champion. We used to socialise a lot, go to parties and have fun. But as he grew older, he got into the gangster image. He was very fiery and wouldn't take a backward step. And later in life, he changed completely. I didn't see it, but everyone said he was using a lot of cocaine. People would look at him the wrong way and he'd attack them. I saw the warning signs early, after our night out at the St Kilda club that almost ended with a fatal shooting. After that, I kept my distance. I respected him, but our friendship was often tested. It was a shame, though, what happened in the end.

Alphonse's father was quite wealthy—he had a travel agency and owned several properties on Lygon Street. Alphonse destroyed all that in his last years. His mother was a beautiful woman who died quite young. As a highly educated kid whose father was in his own business, with money and properties in Carlton, Alphonse had the world at his feet. If he'd chosen the right path he'd be a very successful businessman today. Unfortunately, he chose the other one.

Alphonse made his money in a few ways. He helped people with different problems such as collecting money, and was probably paid by a few places to look after them. He was a big gambler. And he bought and sold things—he sold a lot of his father's properties and was instrumental in destroying much of the family's wealth. He had a couple of trotters; one of them was pretty good. He loved the racing. He also had a share in a King Street nightclub and was involved in fight promotions. [*Gangitano became a promoter of world champion boxer Lester Ellis, who was beaten in the ring by Barry Michael. Not long afterwards, Gangitano attacked the much smaller Michael in a Melbourne nightclub, even trying to bite off the boxer's nose.*]

While we were mates, between Alphonse and me there was always some unspoken competition, a sort of power struggle; we clashed a bit. If we were both sitting at a table and put a cigarette in our mouth, and someone lit my cigarette first, he'd be filthy. Then he wouldn't let anyone light his cigarette—he'd have to light it himself. And if someone shook my hand before his, he'd be furious. Stupid things like that. Several times we fell out and nearly came to blows, although we never actually raised a finger against each other. I had to bar him from the Two-Up, and he didn't speak to me for months after that. He'd pick fights with other customers. If he lost his money, he'd either want to fight someone or to borrow more—and if people didn't lend to him, he'd want to kill them.

One of the *Underbelly* books by journalists John Silvester and Andrew Rule had a story about Chopper Read, quoting him as saying, 'There's only one good bloke in Carlton and that's Mick Gatto'. And he said Alphonse wasn't fit enough to work in a Turkish sauna bath.

Alphonse read it and was frothing at the mouth. I told him I'd paid Chopper $5000 to say it. (I hadn't.)

Apart from being partners in the baccarat in the early 1980s, we never did business together. Even the baccarat was a disaster, especially when I was in jail, because he was either arguing with my brother, John, or threatening and bashing customers. I didn't want to do any more business with him. I just did my own thing, because I knew he was going to be a headache: he was too volatile.

In 1991, Alphonse came to see me in Warrandyte and said he was worried for his wife and daughters. Chopper Read was out of jail. Some years earlier, apparently, Alphonse and a few mates had given it to Chopper, beating him badly. It wasn't one on one, and Chopper was filthy on him. Chopper was a loose cannon. He was running around nightclubs strapped with dynamite, showing people and saying, 'Is Alphonse here?' He was dangerous: he didn't care about going to jail; he didn't care about the police.

Alphonse said, 'I'm worried about the family. I'm thinking about going overseas, but I don't want to go because I don't want people saying, "He was scared and took off"'.

'Alphonse,' I said, 'don't worry about what people think; worry about your family. If you are really worried, my opinion is that you should go'.

So Alphonse went to Italy and the rest of Europe for a few months. He used to ring me all the time, reversing charges, to find out what was going on. It cost me a fortune. [*Gangitano came back to Australia after Read was arrested over other offences and jailed.*]

ALPHONSE

From his early days, Alphonse hated the police, a loathing that began after he got into a fight at a club in Footscray called Bunnys. I wasn't there, but I'm led to believe it was a bloodbath—all the bouncers were attacked and someone drove a car through the front door. The police caught Alphonse, took him back to the station and punched the shit out of him. He told me he was sitting with his hands on a desk when a policeman smashed them with a typewriter. They really battered him. I saw him about a week later: he looked like the Elephant Man, his head was so swollen, and his hands were fucked. It didn't faze him: he copped it on the chin. But he was determined to even up with the coppers that did that to him. I don't know if he ever did.

Alphonse really liked the gangster image. He chased it, going out of his way to meet people with reputations—high-profile crooks from all over Australia. He was quite friendly with Chris Flannery [*a hit man who made his reputation in Sydney in the 1980s, before disappearing, presumed murdered, in May 1985*]. He actually bashed Flannery one night. I don't know what happened. I only met Flannery a few times and had little to do with him. (I couldn't believe he was a hired killer—he looked so insignificant.)

To the best of my knowledge, Graham Kinniburgh never worked with Alphonse. They were friendly, and Graham enjoyed his company. Graham probably controlled him a little bit too. Alphonse used to go to him for advice. If you were a friend of Graham's, you were a friend for life. If you went off the rails, he wouldn't abandon you, and that's how it was with Alphonse. Graham gave him plenty of tongue-lashings, continually telling him that he would end up dead if he continued to stand over people and terrorise them.

Alphonse and Mario Condello clashed a little bit. Once, Mario had a problem with someone in a cake shop, and Alphonse went to the shop and said to the bloke, 'Fuck Mario Condello'. Mario heard about it and was pretty upset, but there wasn't much he could do about it, and it just died. Mario used to stay away from Alphonse.

Alphonse developed a fearful reputation, although some of the stories about him weren't true. One day at the Joker Bar everyone was drunk, having a good time, and this Turkish bloke played up and did the wrong thing. And he copped it in the kneecap. Alphonse was blamed for that but he didn't do it—someone else shot the Turk.

It was also said that Alphonse killed a prostitute who was due to give evidence against Chris Flannery. I don't believe that: I think that was bullshit.

Then there was a story linking him to Jim Pinarkos, who was killed with a crossbow. After Alphonse died, someone put a death notice in the papers that said: 'The impression you left on me will stay forever in my heart—Jim Pinarkos'. I don't believe Alphonse did that killing, either. [*The headless body of Jim Pinarkos was found on Rye Back Beach in July 1989. No one has been charged with the murder.*]

Once, Alphonse shot someone in the leg—a Pommy bloke, a stand-over man that Alphonse was having a power struggle with. I don't know much about it; all I know is that the bloke was being smart and disrespectful and got his right whack.

[*Gangitano was also responsible for shooting dead Greg Workman, a Melbourne criminal, at a party in the early hours of 6 February 1995. Two witnesses to the murder found the police protection system inadequate and changed their police statements, putting Gangitano in the clear. Gangitano then paid for them to fly out of Australia on an extended holiday. The case collapsed, and Gangitano got away with murder.*] I found out about the shooting that day. I had a meeting with Alphonse and he didn't really want to talk too much about it, so I just let it go. It was none of my business.

Several times I saw Alphonse turn on close friends, which left a bad taste in my mouth. I also saw the darker side of him. One night a gorgeous young blonde girl walked past him—she was beautiful—and he said, 'Gee, you're ugly'. He was joking.

She turned around and said, 'Have a look in the mirror yourself'.

And he king-hit her, and broke her nose.

I couldn't believe it. 'You're kidding', I said.

'Fuck her', he said.

That's probably the worst thing I saw Alphonse do. It's something a normal person wouldn't do.

He used to be filthy if someone said something out of order to him, and he acted very quickly. I told my brother to stay away from him, because I knew John was very hot-headed, and wouldn't take a backward step.

A few days before Christmas in 1995, we were at a restaurant in Carlton—there were thirty or forty people there, including the boys from Perth. Alphonse came in with his crew and started drinking. I wasn't really talking to him at the time, so I said hello and left. I didn't want to stay. And that night, Alphonse got into trouble at the Sports Bar, in Melbourne's King Street. [*With Jason Moran and another man, Gangitano attacked and injured thirteen people. Moran was later recorded on a police listening device saying that he had to 'shower to wash the blood off' and that he'd started the fight. Moran was also taped saying about Alphonse: 'He's fucking lulu … If you smash five pool cues and an iron bar over someone's head, you're fucking lulu'. Gangitano was arrested at the scene, but Moran escaped. While police had some evidence against Moran, the case against Gangitano was stronger.*]

Some weeks later, in February 1996, Laurie Connell died. [*Connell was a prominent Western Australian entrepreneur, who set up the Rothwells merchant bank, which later crashed, causing heavy losses to the Western Australian Government and investors. He was investigated by what was known as the WA Inc. Royal Commission, in the early 1990s. He was a prominent racing figure, and was jailed once for conspiracy to pervert the course of justice over a race-fixing incident.*] I didn't know Connell well—only to say, 'Hello, how are you?' But the boys in Perth knew him very well and he was supposed to be a really good bloke. Not long after his death, about ten of us gathered and we held a wake in Melbourne. I got into an argument with a bloke called Kenny; one thing led to another; my brother said something—and it just went bad. Alphonse said he'd been called a liar, then turned on me and wanted to fight me. He ripped his shirt off, abused me and told me to come outside. I was furious. I told him he'd have no luck.

Alphonse had a mate there, too, and Ron Bongetti turned to the bloke and said, 'Keep your hands out of your pockets'. Ronnie had a gun on him. If that bloke had pulled a gun, Ronnie would have shot him—he wouldn't have hesitated. It was getting very nasty. And we were lucky, in a way, because someone reported the argument and the police arrived before anything happened. We went our separate ways. We sorted it out, and ended up mates again. But it just confirmed to me how volatile Alphonse was becoming.

One night in 1996, the bouncers at Monsoons Nightclub wouldn't let Alphonse in, and he threatened to kill them. Someone involved with the bouncers came to see me. They were pretty worried about it. Police pulled him over and they had a blue, and they charged him with threats to kill and God knows what. The organised crime squad raided his house and hit him on the head with the butt of a shotgun.

Towards the end, Alphonse went right off the rails: he was just mad. He got into fights a lot—people would say something and he'd attack them. I've never seen anyone else go off for no reason. And while he wouldn't have made a great prize fighter, he was pretty violent. He did his best to win. [*In 1996, Gangitano reportedly attacked Peter McGauran, a minister in John Howard's government, at Melbourne's prestigious Flower Drum restaurant. McGauran told a News Limited journalist that he was placed in a crushing headlock and punched in the face during a chance encounter. Gangitano said, 'You insulted my friends. Now you will pay'—referring to comment made by McGauran alleging criminal activity in the meat industry. McGauran said he didn't know the identity of his attacker until Gangitano was killed, and his picture appeared on the front pages of newspapers.*]

[*On 16 January 1998, Gangitano was shot dead in his home in Templestowe, in Melbourne's eastern suburbs. He was forty. Police believe the killer was Jason Moran, who put three bullets into Gangitano—who had been his friend—after an argument. Police also believe that Graham Kinniburgh was at the house when the killing happened—he certainly left the house during the evening and returned moments after Gangitano's wife discovered the body. Four years later, the deputy coroner Iain West said that he was satisfied that Kinniburgh*]

and Moran were present at the time of Gangitano's death, but there was insufficient evidence to positively identify the killer.]

I found out early the next morning, when someone rang me. In fact, people thought it was me who'd been killed, because the radio was reporting that a well-known underworld figure had been shot in the eastern suburbs. It didn't take long to work out it was Alphonse. It came as a shock, but I knew it was going to happen one day.

There were hundreds of death notices in the paper, and a big funeral. People flew in from all over Australia for the service. (And there were lots of people there who didn't even know Alphonse, but went along for the ride.) The funeral cars drove slowly down Lygon Street, with people paying their respects. He would have loved it.

Graham had nothing to do with it, as far as I know. He spoke to me about it, but didn't go into detail. He was at the house that night, but wasn't there when the shooting happened. They say Jason killed Alphonse because he'd pleaded guilty to an assault, and that left Jason in a very bad position. (Jason ended up getting two years' jail over it.) There were also stories that Mark Moran (Jason's brother) was there that night. I've heard many rumours and different things. The people who do know are all dead, anyway, so it doesn't make any difference. Who knows? I certainly don't.

I had nothing against Alphonse, and if we fell out we always finished up friends again, and we were mates until the day he died. Alphonse was a good family man. His wife was a good woman who always stayed away from what Alphonse did. She hated it. He had two beautiful daughters, who are now adults. He'd be very proud of them.

13

EASY MONEY

I've known Albanian Sam for many years. He's always out there doing his best, looking for an angle. And he's been a huge punter in his day. One day he called me, excited. 'Mick, I've met these two black blokes. They've got all this money, and want help to invest it. You've got to see this.'

'What do you mean?'

'Mate, hire a hotel room—it'll cost you a couple of hundred dollars. They'll come there and show you. It'll blow your mind.'

I was intrigued, so I agreed. I booked a room at Melbourne's Grand Mercure, where these blokes were already staying, and went with a friend, John.

Sam arrived, and introduced two black men in their early thirties, William and Jonathan. They looked like twins—they were identically dressed in beautiful clothes (Versace), and had matching gold chains and jewellery. They were elegantly spoken, and smart.

Sam said to them, 'These are my friends. Show them the money'.

Both men were wary and wanted the meeting to stop. They looked nervous, and said they only wanted to deal with Sam.

Sam managed to persuade them to stay, although it took a bit of convincing. Finally, William made a phone call up to his room and a third black man—much larger—appeared, carrying a big square silver case. He opened the case. It was lined with what looked like wool, and it was stacked with bank notes. There was only one problem: the notes were all black.

'Pick out a few', Jonathan said.

John picked a couple; Sam picked a couple; and so did I, rummaging at the bottom of the case. The notes were tightly packed—there were lots there.

Jonathan put the black notes onto a hotel plate. The third black man produced a glass vial that he'd kept in the fridge, broke off the end and started rubbing the liquid from it onto the notes. And the next moment, the black notes transformed into US$100 bills. Rinsed under a tap, they were completely clean.

'Have a look at that', I thought.

William and Jonathan said their father, the deputy president of Liberia, had recently been killed. They had fled with their diplomatic passports and several suitcases of cash. They needed someone to provide security for them, and they also wanted help to invest their money in Australia. They had two suitcases with them, each containing US$5 million, and there were another eight suitcases on the way.

William explained that the US Government (through the CIA) had been sending cash to the US-supported Liberian administration, but some of it had been intercepted by rebels. So the CIA had started using a technology that impregnated the cash with a chemical that turned it completely black. This could only be washed off with the chemical 'antidote', which was supplied separately to the Liberians. So when the rebels had next seized the cash, it had been worthless.

The problem, William said, was that he had only a few vials of antidote left, and each vial was good for only about a dozen notes. The one place they could get more antidote was the US embassy, and, before they could even get that, they needed to set up an importing company through the embassy.

'This is our money', William said. 'We own the money and we want to clean the money. But we can't afford to buy the antidote. And we'll get killed if we go back to our own country.' He said it would cost about US$10000 to set up a company. Then it would take a couple of weeks for the antidote to arrive. One litre of antidote cost US$75000 and would clean the contents of one suitcase. He proposed that if we provided short-term security for them and financed the company set-up and the purchase of the antidote, we could keep half of one case's contents—US$2.5 million. From that point on, they would buy their own antidote.

We listened to his story and committed to nothing. We kept the $100 notes that had been washed, and swapped them later for Australian dollars. We all suspected the notes were forgeries, so we took them to a couple of banks and the casino—and we exchanged them without problem. They were authentic.

John told his brother, Tony, about what had happened, and Tony was dismissive. 'It's a scam. Stay away.'

But John was convinced, and managed to arrange another demonstration, where William agreed to use one of the few remaining vials. Tony watched and was stunned, and promptly wanted to become involved. So the four of us—Tony, John, Sam and I—put up the Australian equivalent of US$10000 for William to set up his company through the embassy.

We were still pretty wary and put William under surveillance in case he tried to do a runner. But he didn't, and before long a couple of his cousins arrived in town. Because they had run out of cash, we put them up in a hotel. We also showed them around, looking at properties, cars, investments.

John, meanwhile, started to waver—he was beginning to think it was too good to be true. He was going away for a week's holiday and said he didn't want to be worrying about it while he was overseas. 'I've got a bad feeling about this', he said. 'I'm going to tell them we want our money back. There's something wrong.'

So we saw them.

'We want our money back', John said. 'We're not interested. We think you're crooks, so go and find someone else.'

'Don't be silly', William said, protesting, but he didn't convince John. And they brought back most of the money—they were US$3500 short, but said they couldn't get that back immediately, as the embassy wouldn't refund it, but they would return it to us as soon as possible. We kept tabs on them to ensure we got our money back.

A day or two later, John phoned. He'd had a call from Nick, the owner of a prestige car yard where we'd taken William and Jonathan some days earlier. 'William has ordered two Ferraris. What should we do?'

We thought about it some more. They'd paid us back when we demanded it, and they were acting like they were about to come into big money. We decided we should take a punt and go with it, so we jumped back on board.

We had to wait for the antidote to arrive and, while we waited, we entertained William and Jonathan. They were certainly used to the high life. They stayed in a penthouse at the Paramount, ate at good restaurants, drank expensive wines, received frequent massages, gambled at the casino—and often needed cash for 'living expenses'. We provided all this. Several more cousins had arrived, so there were now about eight of them.

Eventually, the day arrived to pick up the antidote. By this stage we were wary but excited, and a little paranoid. John had become suspicious of a couple of people seen near the bar he owned—he was worried they might be from the CIA. We were also concerned we might be framed or set up for something, so we wanted to do everything within the law.

We arranged for a couple of friends who were surveillance experts to help us follow William and Jonathan to the US embassy on St Kilda Road. We needed to keep a close eye on the suitcases, the antidote, William and Jonathan—and our money. Several of us were involved in the surveillance. We all had radios. As William and Jonathan approached the embassy, Sam spotted a helicopter overhead. He was convinced it was following them and became very concerned that he was about to be arrested. A friend radioed to say there was a high level of security outside the embassy—police were all over the place, as if something was about to happen.

Sam watched as William and Jonathan walked into the embassy, carrying our money. He waited. And waited. About twenty minutes later, they walked out again, carrying a package. Our surveillance team followed as they made their way back to the city penthouse.

When we arrived at the apartment, William handed over an elaborately wrapped bottle. It had US Government labels on it, plus a special seal. Williams said it needed to be refrigerated for seventy-two hours before it would work.

John insisted we try the antidote straightaway.

'It will not work', said William.

'I don't care', said John. 'We are trying it now.'

By this time we had custody of the two suitcases—we had demanded this before handing over the money—but they had combination locks, and we couldn't open them. William unlocked a case and removed a note. We had brought a syringe, and William extracted a small amount of antidote from the bottle, which he put on the note and rubbed in. But instead of becoming clean, the note turned from black to red. William rinsed it under a tap—it was still red, but it was definitely a US$100 note.

'I told you', he said. 'You *must* leave it in the fridge for seventy-two hours. This note is now ruined.'

So we kept the silver cases in our room, and the antidote in our fridge. It was just a matter of time.

Ron Bongetti was assigned to 'look after' William, Jonathan and their friends. (Ron was carrying a gun.) He stayed in the same room as them to make sure they didn't disappear. Ron, though, was in his seventies, and at one stage we found him asleep, so that wasn't much use.

As we began waiting for the seventy-two hours to pass, a phone call came through to William's room, and the black guys went nuts. 'No one is supposed to know about us. We must go.' They were extremely worried. We persuaded them to stay—we could provide the security—and John took them out for dinner. As they walked through the city on the way back to the apartment, an argument broke out in their own language between three of the black guys, and they started fighting. They got seriously stuck into each other, abusing each other. It was unsettling.

That night, John's brother, Tony, was staying with Jonathan. He was like our 'hostage'—we had insisted on this, because we weren't prepared to let these guys out of our sight. But we all felt uncomfortable about it. There were about ten of these black guys by now, and

Tony was a bit exposed. Besides, we had the two cases and the antidote. So we phoned Tony and called him back.

The next morning they had all disappeared. Gone.

The first thing John did was open the fridge and take out the antidote. He pulled off the elaborate wrapping to discover a plastic lemonade bottle. We broke into the two cases and found them full of black pieces of paper. There was no money.

John and I got word that the black guys had moved to another city hotel, and we went down there with a friend we knew who was very willing. We tried to smash open the door and the police were called. It turned out it wasn't William and Jonathan (or their 'cousins'), but some other blokes. So we left it.

Including expenses—and they loved Wagyu beef and the finest wines—we were each down about $45000. Tony, who had been the last to join, had offered to finance the whole deal himself, he had been so confident it would work. He had said we could have equal shares, and he'd take all the risk. I hadn't thought that was fair, and had said we should all chip in. Sometimes I'm just too fair. But eventually Tony did have to come up with the cash, because we were all a bit light on at the time. To do so, he had borrowed the money from my good friend Michael by giving him the title of a Carlton property as security. Tony had planned to ring Michael the day the deal came off, with a coded message: 'We've had a good day'. Michael, of course, didn't get the call.

That night, Tony met Michael to tell him what had happened, although Michael already knew. Tony sat opposite him and burst into tears. Michael sympathised with him—then said he had fourteen days to come up with the money, or he'd keep the property.

Looking back, the black guys were brilliant. They deserved the money, because they played us so well, feeding on our greed. Each time we got suspicious, they drew us back in. The sting was beautiful. There never was any cash in the cases—they simply switched the black pieces of paper we pulled from the cases with authentic pre-blackened notes. It was masterful.

Towards the end, when they needed to make their escape, the phone call had been a set-up, and the street fight had been an act. We were happy Tony didn't stay in the room overnight with one of them—they were capable of slitting his throat or putting something into his drink so that he wouldn't wake up. Tony was lucky (although he didn't think so at the time).

We asked around and discovered that a lot of other people had been conned by them. They had taken some Japanese businessmen for about $400000, and almost got a group of tomato-growers in Cairns for a similar amount.

We learned they were actually from Nigeria, not Liberia, as they had claimed. They concentrated around casinos, where there's black money and gamblers willing to take a risk. There are teams all over the world, constantly getting people.

A couple of weeks afterwards, William phoned me, promising to return our money. I told him we'd hunt him down (although I don't fancy my chances of success). Later, we heard that one of them was locked up by the police in Brisbane, but by the time we found out, he'd disappeared again. There was nothing we could do, so we just left it.

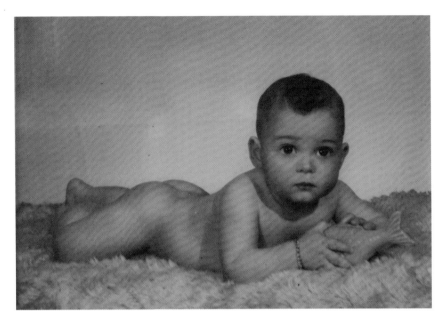

Me as a baby—cute, eh?

Mum and Dad outside our home in South Melbourne. I lived there until I was 21.

Dressed up for another wedding.

Dad at his stall at South Melbourne Market, where I worked as a kid.

Me (left) with Dad and my brother, John.

My last year of school at St Josephs. I was 13. I'm third row from the front, fourth from the left.

A family lunch, with my parents, aunts, uncles and cousins. I'm on the right, smoking.

My fourth pro fight, when I beat Wayne Windahl. We're still mates today.

Ready to rumble, with my trainer Kevin Watterson
(back to camera) and his brothers Phil and Jack (below).

A poster for a ten-round fight in 1977. I was unlucky to lose on points.

With close friend Ange (left) and my brother John.

Marrying Cheryle in 1978 was the best bet I ever made.

My wedding day. Bottom row, from left: Cheryle's father Des, Ron Bongetti, Nappy Ollington, Kevin Watterson and Bruce Johnstone. Middle row, from left: Norm Williams, my best man Ange, and Brian Kane. I'm behind Ange.

With my youngest son Justin, born in 1984, and his sister Sarah.

Outside the L'Alba gambling club in Lygon Street in the 1980s, with Graham Kinniburgh (far left) and Jeff Patterson. Graham later named his pet ferret after Jeff.

With Mario Condello (left) and my brother John. Today, my mobile phone is smaller than the 'brick' on the table.

A night out with friends: from left, Brian, Harry, me, Charlie Wootton and Graham Kinniburgh.

Craig's wedding in Perth in the 1990s was a big night: from right, Mat Tomas, Jason Moran, George Defteros, Graham Kinniburgh, my brother John, me, Jimbo, Tony, and Alphonse Gangitano. The bottom four, from left, are Fat Ange, Dave, Tom Domican and John Kizon.

Above: Uncle Sessel wins again—before I turned him into a starfish.

Left: Gambling has been my life since I was a kid—so I might as well have my own chips!

With Jason Moran and his wife Trisha, and my close friend Steve Kaya.

At Jason Moran's funeral, with (from left) Ron Bongetti, Mat Tomas, Steve Kaya and my brother John (at rear).

Police photographs taken outside La Porcella in Carlton on 23 March 2004. Andrew's Veniamin's silver Mercedes was double-parked on the street.

Left: Andrew Veniamin had a well-deserved reputation for violence. Unfortunately, he tried to kill me and came off second best. (© Newspix/News Ltd)

Home is where the heart is ... with Cheryle on the day of my release.

Celebrating with friends after being found not guilty of murdering Andrew Veniamin. I'd lost 30 kilograms in fourteen months inside. It was a joy to taste good food again.

The media camped outside my home after Mario Condello was murdered. I threw three eggs, and hit three targets.

Loyal friends: (from left) John Khoury, me, John Kizon, Michael, Brian Finn and Mario Condello.

Mario Condello's funeral. We were great friends and his death hit me hard.

I first came across Carl Williams when he was just a kid trying his luck in illegal gambling clubs. He went on to become a dangerous, wealthy drug dealer. (© Richard Cisar-Wright/Newspix)

With former professional kick boxer Sam Greco at his Melbourne café Don Camillo. Sam appeared in the fourth episode of *Underbelly* as nightclub bouncer Bruno Bolotzi.

I have many friends in the union movement, including construction union secretary Bill Oliver.

With Dave 'The Rock' Hedgcock. When he lost his house in the 2009 bushfires, it inspired me to hold a fundraiser.

Jim Bazley was convicted of three 1970s murders linked to the Mr Asia drug syndicate. In 2008, I took him and a few other 'old boys' on a trip to Hong Kong and Macau. They had the time of their lives.

I keep pretty fit, training at home; here I am with my good friend and former pro boxer Frank.

Actor Simon Westaway played me in *Underbelly*. He was stunned when I gave him a pirate copy of the series before it went to air.

My eldest son Damien works at Elite Cranes. He was also a handy footballer.

My youngest son Justin was lucky to survive a horror car accident in 2007.

I was so proud when I walked my daughter Sarah down the aisle in February 2009. She and her husband Regan make a wonderful couple.

Proud grandparents. My grandson is also called Dominic Gatto, but he won't be following in my footsteps.

After more than 30 years of marriage, Cheryle and I are still going strong.

More than 1100 people came to support a fundraising dinner at Melbourne's Docklands, including volunteer fire fighters.

Presenting a cheque to Country Fire Authority chief Neil Bibby, three weeks after the bushfire fundraiser. It was a proud moment.

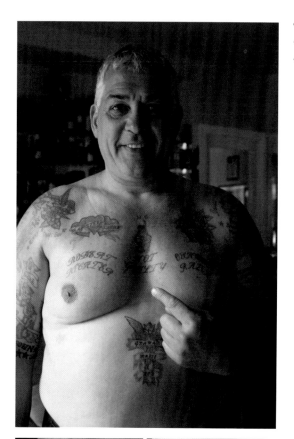

The tattoos tell the story: 'Robert Richter', 'Not Guilty', 'Ockams Razor'.

My 'dead legs': on my calf muscles are tattoos created by a brilliant artist in North Melbourne in memory of Graham Kinniburgh, my dad, Mario Condello and Ron Bongetti.

EASY MONEY

At the start of the exercise, we had offered a share to my good friend Michael. He had wished us luck, said he hoped it worked out, but wouldn't be swayed further than lending Tony the money, backed with security. And Michael's advice to me is the moral to this story: if it looks too good to be true, it probably is.

14

THE WARS BEGIN

A lot has been written about the Gangland Wars, and many people watched them through the TV show *Underbelly*. In reality, the Gangland Wars involved about fifteen killings, and not the thirty-odd that some people have claimed. They've tied things into the 'wars' that had nothing to do with them, probably to make them sound better. The police also encouraged this, so some of them won promotions and got better resources. Never let the truth get in the way of a good story.

The truth is, the wars started on 13 October 1999, the day Carl Williams was shot in a suburban park.

I first came across Carl when he was quite young, when he came to the Two-Up with his father, George. Carl's dad was just a knockabout and they were doing their best. Carl would have a bet and try to get a dollar. He used to be broke and desperate. He was always a happy-go-lucky sort of bloke, but just nothing—an insignificant face in the crowd. He used to come in, have a couple of bets, do his money, and we'd give him the cab fare to get home. I used to bump into him from time to time, and it was just 'Hello, how are you?'

I heard about the shooting not long after it happened, but it meant nothing to me. The rumour was that the shooting was over drugs or money owing—I remember a figure of $400000 being mentioned. I was aware that party drugs were in every nightclub, but I'd stopped going to clubs years earlier. I remember wondering why the gunmen hadn't killed him.

It's common knowledge that Jason and Mark Moran did it. And they should have killed him. It was a huge mistake. If they had put him out of his misery, there would be quite a few people still alive today, among them some of my good friends. Having said that, I'm a firm believer in 'an eye for an eye'. If someone does harm to you or your family, you're entitled to even the score. I know the general public might not believe in that, but I do. So Carl was well within his rights to seek revenge.

Unfortunately, Carl made a lot of money out of drugs and became very dangerous. He surrounded himself with people who poisoned his brain. That's when he started putting money out for different people to be killed. If he was still running free today, I've no doubt there would be another thirty people dead, including my family and more of my friends. He was never going to stop.

I was a teenager when I first met Lewis Moran: he ran around with Brian Kane, and was good friends with Graham Kinniburgh. Lewis was a slaughterman and boner. He was also an SP bookmaker and had people work for him on commission. And he was a very good pickpocket, one of the best around town. If he went to Caulfield

Racecourse for the day, it wouldn't be unusual for him to finish up with twenty or thirty wallets. He was very, very good. One of his loves in life was cooking—he liked watching cooking shows on television. Over the years, I went to his joint a few times for a meal, and it was always great.

I had a lot of time for Lewis, but we weren't as close as people think. We had dinner a few times, but not often. He called in to La Porcella once in a blue moon for a coffee, and we often talked about gambling. He introduced me to a couple of bookies I used to bet with, and sometimes I'd ring him for tips. But we did very little business together. Lewis and I had great respect for each other. Although we saw each other rarely, if he could help me, he would—and if I could help him, I would. We had that sort of relationship. What he did was his business, and it had nothing to do with me.

I knew his sons, Jason (who married Brian Kane's niece, Trish) and Mark. Jason was a 'red light'—he attracted trouble. He had run around with Alphonse causing mayhem, attracting all sorts of attention. I had little to do with him. I saw a bit of Mark: I liked him because there was no shit in him. He was serious, and straight up and down. What you saw was what you got. He was a fitness fanatic. I used to train at Melbourne's Underworld Gym, and sometimes he'd be there too. He did weights and I did boxing—we were in different areas of the gym, but we used to bump into each other. He was always a pleasant, quiet, shy sort of bloke who never looked for trouble. We'd have a yak for five minutes then go our own way. Whenever we met, it'd just be a few words and that'd be it. I might bump into him at a party or a funeral. At one time he was an SP bookmaker and I had a few bets with him. But we ran in different circles.

On the night of 15 June 2000, Lewis rang me. 'They've just killed Mark', he said. 'They shot him in front of his house.'

I couldn't believe it.

'Can you come over?' said Lewis. 'Do you mind coming over?'

So I shot across to Mark's home in Aberfeldie, in Melbourne's northern suburbs. I think I went with Ron Bongetti.

The streets were cordoned off, and I said to a copper, 'Lewis rang me. My name's Mick Gatto. He wants me to go and see him'. They rang whoever was in charge and let me through. I went in and gave Lewis a hug. His immediate family was there, and it was shocking, terrible. The family were devastated. Mark was still outside in the car. They left his body there for hours while they did their forensic tests.

At the time, I don't think Lewis had any idea who'd done it. He certainly didn't think it was Carl Williams. There's one thing that is pretty certain—Carl financed the killing. But he didn't do it himself. That's a guarantee. I know a witness put him there, but it's not true. I'm confident Carl didn't do it. He hasn't got the dash.

[*Two guns—a twelve-gauge shotgun and a handgun—were used to kill Moran, who was shot in the chest as he was getting into his utility. A coronial inquest said he may have been shot by one person or more. No charges have ever been laid. There is no doubt, however, that Carl Williams was behind the killing, taking revenge for his shooting months earlier. There were strong suggestions by a protected witness, whose name is suppressed, that Williams was present at the shooting, either as the getaway driver or as a gunman.*]

After Mark died, several stories circulated that were rubbish. The silliest one tied Mark to Richard Mladenic, saying Richard was Mark's bodyguard. That was all nonsense. Richard wasn't Mark's bodyguard; in fact, I don't know if Mark had anything to do with him at all.

Richard was as mad as a rattlesnake. I quite liked him, but he was mad. He had done a heap of jail, and would fight anyone, coppers included. At the same time, he was very smart, and wrote beautiful poetry.

I came across him years ago, in Lygon Street. He was a big, strapping young bloke, fit as a fiddle. He used to go into restaurants and terrorise people, stand over them. He'd say, 'I'll come back with a bazooka and blow the fucking joint up'.

He was doing this to friends of mine. I was forever grabbing him, saying, 'Mate, pull up'.

'Oh, Mick, I'm sorry', he'd say. 'I didn't know they were friends of yours.' And he'd go back and apologise to them.

People were terrified of him. But he was more of a pest than anything else. No one would have him as a bodyguard—he was too mad—and certainly not Mark Moran. Mark was always under the radar, low-key, someone who looked after his gang and did what needed to be done nice and quietly. Having a lunatic like Richard as part of that was nonsense.

[*On 16 May 2000, Richard Mladenic was shot dead in a St Kilda motel room.*] I don't know why he got killed, although I've heard all sorts of rumours. I was surprised when I heard. I thought of him as a mad hatter, but harmless.

15

ANDREW

Andrew 'Benji' Veniamin was ambitious. When I first met him, in about 2001, he already had a reputation for violence. By then he'd apparently killed three men. Before he died, he killed three more and was involved in the torture and murder of a seventh. Not to mention other suspected murders, or the bashings and shootings. All by the age of twenty-eight.

Andrew's apparent murder victims—including a few people that I knew—were:

Joe Quadara [*shot outside a Toorak supermarket in May 1999*]. I knew Joe: I sometimes saw him at the markets, and I'd say, 'Hello, how are you?' I knew his brothers and his sister quite well. He knew my father and my family. It was a pretty big shock in our circle that he was killed, because he ran a quiet life. I often thought he was killed by mistake.

Frank Benvenuto [*shot outside his Beaumaris home in May 2000*]. I knew Frank quite well, having known the family for years from the markets. I don't know why he was killed, although it may have been because he owed money.

Dino Dibra [*shot near his West Sunshine home in October 2000*]. I never actually met Dino, but once saw him outside a car yard in North Melbourne. He was in a car doing wheelies, and dropping donuts out the front of the joint. Apparently he had some problem with one of the blokes at the car yard. I didn't go into it, because it was nothing to do with me.

Victor Peirce [*shot in his car in Port Melbourne in May 2002*]. I met Victor through Frank Benvenuto. He was said to have been behind the killing of two police in Walsh Street in 1988. I met him a few times for a coffee—he usually wanted to borrow money. I liked him. There were different rumours about why he was killed, but I have no idea.

Paul Kallipolitis [*shot in his Sunshine home in October 2002*]. I met Paul once outside a Carlton restaurant, when he was introduced to me by a friend. We shook hands and that was it. Not long afterwards he got killed. They say he was a lunatic, pretty volatile. The rumour was that he was standing over people, running in and taking over other people's drug crops. He was running pretty hot.

Nik Radev [*shot in Coburg in April 2003*]. I met Nik a few times. I didn't like him: he was always very aggressive—not towards me—it was just his nature. He'd done a lot of jail.

Mark Mallia [*whose burned remains were found in a drain in West Sunshine in August 2003—Veniamin reportedly took part in his torture*]. I didn't know Mallia.

ANDREW

Andrew was pretty wild. There was an incident at Digger's Rest where he shot some bloke in the legs. Another man out Geelong way was waiting for Andrew one morning at the bus stop. Andrew drove up and put a few into him, shooting him in the legs and buttocks. I don't know what it was about—it may have been drug-related.

A bloke called Pasquale Zaffina had problems, too. (He gave evidence at my trial.) Andrew started going out with Zaffina's girlfriend, and they had a dispute. Andrew went to Zaffina's parents' house, shot it up and put some sort of explosive device at the front—it didn't go off—and then threatened to kill this bloke's sister. So Zaffina said they should meet in a park and have a punch-on: the best man wins. And they agreed there would be no guns. But before the first punch was thrown, Andrew produced a .38 from the back of his pants and started shooting, hitting Zaffina two or three times in the leg. It was great evidence in my trial, because Andrew was wearing similar clothes on the day he died, and pulled a concealed gun from his pants.

Andrew attracted police attention, and one day they raided his home in Sunshine, finding a .38 handgun hidden in a secret compartment under the kitchen sink. He said it wasn't his; it was his mother's. He also said some jewellery had gone missing.

He went mad, and told my friend Steve that he was going to a police station to shoot the coppers in revenge. He didn't care if he was killed—he just wanted to get eight or ten coppers. Steve managed to calm him down and stop him going through with it, although it was a close thing. Andrew was ready to go.

When I met him, I'd heard the rumours, but I didn't know if they were true. In one of our first meetings, at a Lygon Street restaurant,

I put my arm around his shoulder and felt the butt of the handle of a gun. 'Oh, you're loaded', I said, and he laughed. He used to carry a gun quite often.

Early one morning—about 2 a.m.—a few of us were having a late snack at a 24-hour restaurant in Carlton. Normally I would have been home in bed, but we'd been out that night, maybe to the fights, and were having something to eat.

Steve Kaya, who is one of my true loyal friends, was with us, and his phone rang. It was Andrew—Steve was a close friend of his too—and Andrew said he was at the Men's Gallery strip club in the city and that the bouncers were trying to belt him.

I said, 'Come on; we'll fly down and see if we can help him'. So we jumped into a couple of cars and drove there. We went to see what was going on, and if we could pull it up. I didn't want him belted. He was a friend, plus he was only a little bloke. As soon as we pulled up and he saw us, he started attacking the bouncers! I stepped in to try to control him—it was crazy.

I knew most of the owners of the nightclubs, and a lot of the security staff, so Andrew knew there was a fair chance I could diffuse things if they got out of control.

A couple of times, Andrew came to the kickboxing, which I usually watched with a group of friends. Tarik Solak was the promoter (he's a great bloke) so we'd get top seats. It was fun, plenty of razzamatazz and good fights. Tarik always put on a show. Andrew had fought both as a kickboxer and a boxer, and enjoyed the nights out. They say he wasn't a bad fighter, but then he had a motorbike accident and did his knee, and he couldn't fight any more.

Andrew also came to my son Damien's twenty-first birthday at the Metro Nightclub—along with 600 other people. A couple of knockabouts in the crowd joked that night: 'Mick, you've given the police a night off, because all the crooks are here'.

I was asked at my trial why I would want to be involved with a killer like Andrew. The answer was simple—I'm a networker. I believe in knowing a wide range of people from all walks of life. What they do is their business, as long as it doesn't affect me. It can be handy. And with Andrew, I thought one day I could use it to my advantage if I had a problem in Melbourne's western suburbs (where he was from) and I needed some local knowledge.

But in the end, I never did any business with Andrew, although he always wanted me to find him work. We simply worked in different areas.

'Mate, I'll get you a job on a building site', I'd say.

'No, I want to make big money.'

'I'm sort of in the building trade and I can help you that way. But I'm not into drugs and things of that nature, where there's big money involved. It's not my cup of tea, Andrew.'

'Mate, I'll do anything.'

'I'll find you a job as a labourer.'

But he didn't want to work, and I certainly didn't want anyone hurt, or killed or anything like that.

I used to see Andrew maybe once a week, once a fortnight, whenever he came in to talk to the boys. We used to speak on the phone now and then, but I never had a great deal to do with him. The friendship was really one-way. I was forever getting him out of trouble, and he was forever asking for my advice and help.

Andrew was always broke, and a couple of times I gave him $5000 to kick along with. He also used to get awfully depressed. He would see me and say, 'I'm sick of this. I've had enough. I'm going away: I'm going to move overseas. I've got no money'. Later, when he teamed up with Carl Williams, he found the big money he was after.

In August 2003, Andrew was one of about fifty blokes who came to my forty-eighth birthday party. It was a surprise party at a Lygon Street restaurant, and I think Ron Bongetti rang him. (I knew about the party, but not who was coming.) And that night Andrew had a few drinks—one of the rare occasions I saw him drink. He usually avoided alcohol and just drank water.

I'd heard the rumours about him killing two of his good friends—Dino Dibra and Paul Kallipolitis—so I thought I'd ask him about them. I waved him over to a quiet corner, where we stood alone. 'I've got to ask you', I said. 'All these rumours about you killing Dibra and PK—what's the story with that?'

'Mick,' he said, 'they were dogs. They deserved what they got'. He went on to say they'd fallen out. 'And I should have put another clip in Dibra: he deserved it.'

I was quite shocked—not just that he'd killed his best mates, but that he'd talk about it. He wasn't the type to brag, and always played it close to his chest. He never said much to anyone, even to those people who'd known him all his life—which was why I was so surprised. I'd expected him to laugh off my question. It makes me wonder about the testimony of some police informers, who claim now that Andrew told them all about his activities. In one case it's clearly bullshit, because I know Andrew didn't like or trust the bloke who is telling the stories. Andrew's brother, his family, his friends—they would say the same thing. He simply wouldn't brag to someone who didn't need to know about it.

Andrew became a loose cannon, capable of anything. If the money was right, he'd kill anyone; that's what he was like. And he had his fair share of supporters, people on his team. But today, a lot of those people hate him. They found out what he was doing behind their backs, including those friends of his in jail. While they were inside, he was on with their wives, on with their girlfriends. He lost a lot of support. Towards the end, he was just running amok, going around town standing over people. One night there was a fight at the casino, and Andrew tried to stand over this bloke—a mate of mine—threatening to harm him, harm his family. He was demanding $100 000. It was madness. If you do that sort of thing in Melbourne there are only two ways you finish—in jail or in a hole (and he finished in a hole).

16

THE MEDITERRANEAN

I met The Mediterranean [*who can't be named for legal reasons*] in the 1980s, when he and his brother (who I'll call Harry) played cards at gambling clubs in Carlton. We became friends and there was never a problem. The Mediterranean was a good bloke, very showy, had a bit of charisma about him. I'd always liked him. I knew what sort of business he was in—drugs—and he knew I stayed away from it. Every now and then I'd bump into him and we'd have something to eat. He used to always call me 'Champion'. Harry, who I was closer to, was a real gentleman.

By the late 1990s, The Mediterranean had made a lot of money. People say he had a 'green light' [*police backing*] and could do what he liked, including selling drugs from the back of his car—in front of a police station.

[*In 2002, The Mediterranean was arrested and charged with drug trafficking. At about the same time, serious corruption in the Victoria Police drug squad began to be revealed publicly, and affected a series of criminal cases. Drug charges were dropped against several accused, because of concerns about the evidence. Over a matter of months, a number of prominent suspected drug dealers were let out, including Carl Williams. In September 2003, The Mediterranean was released from jail because an unresolved probe into police corruption had continually delayed his prosecution. He was bailed, and allowed to be in the community until his case came up.*]

My dad was a wise man who told me many things. He warned me away from certain Italian people—'Don't go near him'—and told me to mind my own business. 'If you mind your own business, you won't get into trouble', he said. If I'd remembered his advice, it would have saved me a lot of grief. Instead, I ended up doing what I thought was the right thing—and walked into the middle of someone else's argument.

The problem began when a little bloke called Rocky sent a message to a couple of the boys in Perth, Troy and Fab, saying that while he was in jail The Mediterranean had been calling them 'dogs'. To call someone a dog is one of the worst insults possible. It suggests you are untrustworthy, a police informer, a low-life. The boys from Perth weren't impressed. They wanted this sorted out. And when The Mediterranean was released from jail, they decided to fly to Melbourne for a meeting to resolve the issue. They asked a bloke called Ange to be the conduit, but he was a bit smart. 'Mick can organise that', he said, handballing it to me.

For years I've had good friends in Perth. These days I get there once or twice a year, and enjoy going there. I'm close to John Kizon, who is an absolute gentleman—he knew me from Melbourne when we were young. After I was arrested and charged with killing Andrew

Veniamin, John was on the phone every day, supporting my wife and kids, anything he could do. He's a brilliant bloke and a very good friend. He has introduced me to some great guys in Perth, such as Troy, Craig, Fab and Jack. They are all colourful characters who do their own thing, and my association with them has been purely friendship—there's no business involved.

Unfortunately, John is Public Enemy No. 1 in Perth, and the authorities drive him mad. He was convicted over a small amount of heroin when he was eighteen—and it wasn't even his. It belonged to the other bloke in the car, but John copped the rap and now has to live with it for the rest of his life. It's his greatest regret, being in that car with that bloke. Years later, he's still branded a drug dealer and treated like a common criminal. Yet he's a businessman who does a lot of work in Indonesia, where he's treated with great respect. As far as I know he's had no involvement in drugs. There was a huge Australia-wide investigation that looked at him, me and many others, and went for a long time. We were under 24-hour surveillance—phone taps, everything—and nothing came of it except innuendos. No charges. It was a huge waste of taxpayers' money.

So when Troy and Fab from Perth asked me to help set up the meeting, I said I would. It was simply a matter of having a meeting, getting an apology and making peace. I spoke to Harry and told him the story—'All your brother's got to do is come here on his own, apologise, say he's sorry, that he didn't mean it, and that'll be the end of it'. Harry spoke to his brother, and said that was fine. He'd come and say sorry.

It was a beautiful November day. A group of us were sitting outside La Porcella at a big table in the sunshine. Most Fridays, a group of us would have lunch there—sometimes they might cook a whole pig. It was usually a fun day. This particular lunchtime there were perhaps twenty of us. Andrew Veniamin happened to pop in that day. Mario Condello was there too. And there was the head of a union and a couple of businessmen.

I rang Harry to check his brother was coming over. 'For God's sake,' I said, 'tell him not to get smart. He just needs to apologise—that's all he's got to do'.

'Yeah, no problem', said Harry. 'That'll happen.'

But the moment The Mediterranean arrived I could see there was a problem. He was really being smart, showing off, and he had a go at Ange. I don't know if he was on something, but he was very aggressive.

I grabbed him and the boys from Perth and we walked around the corner. If he was going to apologise, I didn't want to embarrass him in front of other people.

I introduced them, and waited for the apology.

Troy began. 'I hear you been calling me a dog.'

'Well, you are, aren't you?'

I went white. I couldn't believe what came out of The Mediterranean's mouth. And I knew there was no way out of it then.

Troy went right up to The Mediterranean and put his forehead to The Mediterranean's forehead. 'What? Are you calling me a dog?'

'Yeah, you're a dog.'

The next moment, Troy clocked him. He had no choice. He would have been weak in my eyes—and his own eyes—if he hadn't retaliated.

Some damage was done when The Mediterranean fell on the ground. Then he stuck his head up and someone kicked him right in the head, and that caused a fair bit more damage. Big Jack, who had come with The Mediterranean, tried his best to help, and he got involved in the fight. But it just happened so quickly. I tried my best to stop it, but Troy and Fab were furious, and I don't blame them. The Mediterranean copped a severe kicking.

The people at the table heard the commotion—they didn't witness it, but they saw the bloody aftermath. I told some of them they should move. 'You'd better go: the coppers are going to come; it'll be all over the news.' [*Surprisingly, the police didn't hear about the incident for some time, and the bashing didn't make the news.*]

I took The Mediterranean into the bathroom so he could wash his face and clean up. I was angry that he'd come to the meeting and not done the right thing. 'Mate, you were out of order. You were supposed to come here and apologise, and instead you get smart with them. What did you put me in that position for?'

And he got a bit upset. 'I've copped a belting, and now you're going to give me a spray?'

'Yeah, I am, because you put me in a bad position', I said. 'I'm trying to do you all a favour by rectifying this problem, and you've created a bigger problem.'

Someone needed to take The Mediterranean to a doctor, so I asked Andrew Veniamin. 'Andrew, do us a favour—take him and get him patched up', I said. (We had a doctor sweet, who would treat the injuries discreetly.) And off they went. This also introduced Andrew to The Mediterranean—before long they'd formed a tight working relationship. Andrew also became close to Carl Williams through The Mediterranean, and as a result more people died at Andrew's hands. They both offered Andrew easy drug money, which I couldn't. There was big money there, and Andrew tapped into it.

From that day onwards, The Mediterranean had this insane belief that I had set him up. Deep in his heart he couldn't possibly have believed it. But he was filthy on the fact that not only did he get belted—there was blood everywhere—but I'd yelled at him. It hurt his pride.

We had a meeting some time later and I told him again that I hadn't set him up, but he didn't believe me. His brother, Harry, sided with me, saying, 'If Mick had set you up, you wouldn't have walked away'. Harry was embarrassed by his brother's behaviour. And the brothers fell out over the incident and didn't speak for a couple of years.

The Mediterranean subsequently put out a contract to have me killed. Some coppers told me about it, as did different knockabouts I knew. There was no doubt there was a contract on me, but I don't know how serious it was. I went and saw The Mediterranean and asked him, and he denied it.

But I know that Nik Radev was offered $400000 to kill me—his plan was to drive past La Porcella with another man on a motorcycle, and shoot me with a machine gun. Radev kept asking for a $50000 upfront fee, but The Mediterranean wouldn't put the money up. If he had, Radev might have acted on it.

In the end, the contract wasn't taken up. One reason was that Nik Radev's body finished up riddled with bullets.

17

THE KILLING FIELDS

Melbourne's Gangland Wars continued after the wounding of Carl Williams, in November 1999, with the deadly revenge shooting of Mark Moran in June 2000. Between 2000 and 2002, Andrew Veniamin was the reputed killer in four murders: Frank Benvenuto, Dino Dibra, Victor Peirce and Paul Kallipolitis. But it wasn't until 2003 that the police—and the public—really took notice of what was going on.

The first victim of 2003 was Nik Radev. I'd met Nik a few times—he'd come into La Porcella—and I wasn't a fan. He was arrogant, and aggressive in the way he talked and acted, probably because of all the jail time he'd done. He always treated me with respect, but I didn't like him. He was killed in Coburg. It's been proven that Andrew killed him [*together with another man who cannot be named for legal reasons*]. They both emptied their guns into him. [*Radev was a Bulgarian ex-wrestler who reportedly arrived in Australia in 1980 as a refugee—and within five years was jailed for drug trafficking. He worked as a violent standover man and drug dealer and, by 2003, was supposedly becoming too ambitious, with his eyes on a new slice of*

Melbourne's lucrative 'party pills' market. Carl Williams was strongly suspected of ordering and financing Radev's murder, although he was never charged. Radev was buried in a gold-plated casket that cost some $30000.]

But it was the killing two months later of Jason Moran in front of his children at a football ground that got the public's attention. For many years, Jason had been a loose cannon, always playing up, getting into trouble and fighting. He was quick-tempered and very violent. And he wasn't a good fighter—he was just violent. He'd grab anything, do anything, bite and scratch.

Even though I'd known him for years, I didn't spend time with him because he attracted trouble. I had a family and didn't want to finish up in jail or dead. But in the year leading up to his death, I saw a bit of him and got to know him better—he'd mellowed and become more of a family man. He was also very cautious. Once Carl Williams was released from jail in July 2002, Jason knew he might be in trouble, so he took extra precautions. [*Williams was released after fourteen months in custody because of delays in prosecuting his case.*]

Everyone knew Jason was a possible target—his brother, Mark, had been killed in revenge for shooting Carl, and it didn't take much to work out who might be next. There were rumours that Carl's team might kill Jason's father, Lewis, or kill Jason when he drove to visit Lewis at Port Phillip Prison. [*At the time, Lewis Moran was in custody on drugs charges.*] I made sure I got a message to Carl, through Andrew, that if he had problems with Lewis and Jason, that was his business. But I knew Graham Kinniburgh sometimes drove with Jason to visit Lewis in jail, and I wanted to make sure Carl didn't ambush Jason's car if Graham was on board. My message was blunt: 'I don't care what you do, but leave Graham alone'.

[*On 21 June 2003, Jason Moran and a friend, Pasquale Barbaro, were shot dead as they sat in a van at a game of junior football in*

Essendon North. The gunman used a shotgun to blast Moran, who was in the driver's seat, then followed up with a handgun. Barbaro, in the passenger seat, was also hit and killed. Inside the van during the shooting were at least five children, including Moran's six-year-old twins. Several other children were playing nearby.] The police had a whiteboard with the names of victims and suspects, but they only got serious when Jason was killed in front of all those kids and there was a massive public outcry. If that hadn't happened, the tit-for-tat shootings would have kept going, and the police would have sat on the fence. For them, it was only crims killing each other. Most police didn't care: it was cleaning things up for them. But that shooting was what turned it around, and the police decided to get off their arse and do something. [*Victoria Police set up the Purana taskforce to investigate underworld killings a month before Moran and Barbaro were killed. Carl Williams later pleaded guilty to financing Moran's murder, in revenge for being shot in a suburban park more than three years earlier. The shooter, a man who cannot be identified but who is known as The Runner, was also convicted of the killing.*]

It was a very low act, in front of children like that. It's just not the right way to go about things. The kids in that car could have been hit by pellets from the shotgun. It was a very, very bad killing. They could have killed Jason a million other ways. The kids are scarred for life—and there were kids in that van who had nothing to do with the Morans. That sort of behaviour comes back to haunt you.

Lewis was in jail when Jason was shot, and the authorities didn't let him attend his son's funeral. It was a sad affair.

One side issue from Jason's murder was a death notice placed in Melbourne's *Herald Sun* newspaper that said, in part: 'Moran, Jason, RIP. Thirty pieces of silver. Respect to all the poor little kiddies'. It was 'signed' by a number of people, including Andrew, Carl Williams and his father—and me! My 'signature' was 'Mick "The Don" Gatto'.

I haven't found out who put that notice in, but I could have a good guess. Apart from aligning me with that message and those people, it was the first time I'd ever seen my name associated with 'The Don'—no one had ever called me that before. But, unfortunately, it seems to have stuck. [*Three other men, who cannot be named for legal reasons, were also 'signatories' to the notice.*]

A month after Jason Moran and Pasquale Barbaro were cut down, Willie Thomson was shot in his car at Chadstone. I knew Willie quite well, and I liked him. We'd known each other for about fifteen years. He'd been into martial arts, plus he'd done a bit of acting. While he was a pretty easy-going bloke, he was also quite ambitious. He talked to me a fair bit about putting vending machines into nightclubs (selling everything from soft drinks to condoms). He came up with a series of different schemes to make money, although in the end we never did any business together. There were stories that he dabbled in drugs, but I didn't realise he was heavily involved.

When he was killed I was quite surprised, because I thought he was an insignificant player. There was obviously more to his murder than meets the eye. I heard different rumours about why he was killed. One was that he owed a lot of money to certain people and they got rid of him because he wouldn't pay. Another was that he had a heap of drugs and they took them and killed him. Another was that he was owed a lot of money, so he was killed to 'square the debt'. I don't know which one's right. Carl Williams was blamed for the murder.

The following month, the charred remains of Mark Mallia, aged thirty, were found in a drain in West Sunshine. He was apparently identified by a tattoo on his shoulder. I didn't know him, but he was one of Carl's growing list of victims. [*Mallia was associated with Nik Radev, and may have been ready to take revenge for Radev's murder four months earlier. According to evidence given in court, Mallia was kidnapped and tied to a chair in the garage of a suburban home, where he was tortured. During the torture, Carl Williams came to visit and see the victim, and paid $50 000 in cash for him to be killed. Williams pleaded guilty to being behind the murder of Mallia—he did it, apparently, because Mallia presented a threat.*]

During the Gangland Wars, it was important to keep a sense of humour. On a warm night late in 2003, a large group of us had dinner in Carlton. Mario Condello didn't want to come because Lewis Moran was going to be there, and rumour had it that Lewis was a target. In the end, Mario came, wearing a bullet-proof vest under his coat—and when he walked into the restaurant he made sure he sat at the opposite end of the table to Lewis. Ron Bongetti was there, sweating, because he had to wear his jacket all night (he was carrying). A few others came too, including Graham Kinniburgh.

One of those at dinner was a friend called Tony, who was a hugely successful businessman in the retail world. We often joke about how Tony turned a big business into a little business through gambling. His kids have since taken the business over and turned it around. Tony was delightfully naïve about criminals and the underworld. On one occasion, he had met a very good thief, but had no idea who he was or what he did. They started chatting and the thief told Tony he was in the 'iron and steel' business (shorthand for 'My wife irons and I steal'). But Tony believed him. The thief told Tony he was selling suits from the boot of his car, and Tony said, 'Mate, as the business picks up, you should think about opening up a shop'. Tony didn't realise the suits were hot.

As the evening came towards an end, Lewis said he'd grab a cab home. Tony offered him a lift! No one else wanted to be in a car with Lewis, but Tony had no idea what was happening under the surface. In the end, Tony took Lewis back to his place and they both got home okay.

Another day, police pulled me over as I was driving. They were from the Purana taskforce, investigating the gangland murders, and wanted to search the vehicle.

'Go for your life', I said.

They went through the car and, in the boot, found my briefcase. Inside was a gun. 'What's this?' they said.

I could see they were pretty happy. But it was a plastic toy gun my son had given me. I showed them, and they gave it back.

Then one of them emerged from the front console with a small bag of white powder. 'And what's this?'

I blew up. 'Don't you bastards load me [*plant evidence*]. You know I hate drugs.'

'I'm sorry, sir. You're going to have to park the car properly and come back with us to the station, where we'll analyse the powder.'

I was furious. I rang my lawyer, then parked. As I did so, I saw in the car some caps that went in an exploding toy pen (which has made a few people jump, including Melbourne's Lord Mayor Robert

Doyle). And suddenly I realised what the white powder was. I got out of the car. 'Listen, I really owe you people an apology', I said.

'What for?'

'I thought you were setting me up with drugs, but I was wrong. That's itching powder. I got it from the trick shop.' And I explained that I liked playing practical jokes and had been putting the powder in Ron Bongetti's bed when he wasn't looking—and he would blame the air-conditioning because he was tossing and turning. (He later found out and got me back.) I told them I was happy to go to the station if the powder needed to be analysed.

They opened the packet, checked the contents and were satisfied.

In October 2003, Michael Marshall was shot dead in the street, in front of his five-year-old son. I'd never met Marshall. It was another shocking incident, killing a man in front of a child. That stuff used to be taboo. [*Police listened to the killing, having bugged the van being used by the gunmen, and arrested both men soon afterwards. The identity of the killers cannot be revealed for legal reasons, although one was The Runner, who was also responsible for killing Jason Moran.*] I knew The Runner quite well—he often came to the Two-Up. He had a reputation as a good armed robber and a runner. I didn't mind him—until he did those shootings in front of all those kids.

Many years ago, The Runner had a dispute with a mate of mine from the Two-Up, who was a boxer—he was a very good bloke, had never been in trouble. So when The Runner threatened to kill him, he was not surprisingly a little nervous, especially after he saw

The Runner driving past his house a few times. This bloke was also a good shooter—he used to go hunting all the time—so he loaded a .303 rifle and, the next time The Runner drove past, he put one into the middle pillar of the car between the two windows. The Runner never went back.

The killing of Michael Marshall was the sixth murder in a six-month period—five of them in public places, and three of them in front of children. And, for me, the worst was yet to come.

18

GRAHAM

I met Graham Kinniburgh when I was about sixteen. He ran around with quite a few blokes, including brothers Brian and Les Kane— their crew had a pretty big reputation in town. In those early days Graham was very standoffish; it was hard to get close to him. It took a few years for us to build our friendship, and we became great friends. Of all those people who died in the Gangland Wars, I miss Graham the most.

He was an excellent safe-cutter and that was what he concentrated on. Every time a new safe was made, he would buy one, dissect it, analyse it and work out how to get into it. That was his business. In the 1990s, security and surveillance became too good, so he stopped. He didn't believe in harming or terrorising people, so never really liked armed robberies. He often said—and the words stuck in my head—'Never ask anyone to do something that you're not prepared to do yourself'. There's a movie called *Enemy of the State*, with Gene Hackman. That character reminded me so much of Graham it was unbelievable—secretive, technically smart and switched on—and they even looked similar.

We did a lot of things together, often with duplicate keys. Then after I went to jail in 1982, I didn't do much with him. Every now and then, if there was something cooking, I'd be involved. But it wasn't much.

A few times in the early 1980s he threw a bundle of money to me, for no reason. 'Mate, this is for you.'

'What for?'

'We did something. You're down on your luck, so this is for you.'

And that was it—he'd never tell me what he'd done or where the money was from. And I learned not to ask. He was very secretive and wouldn't let his left hand know what his right hand was doing. If he did something, he simply wouldn't tell you about it. He was tied up in the Magnetic Drill Gang, which took millions from safes. But he wouldn't discuss it. If you asked him (and I tried), he'd just laugh and wouldn't say anything. He was a smart bugger.

Our wedding anniversaries fell on nearly the same date, so every year we'd go with our wives to a restaurant (often Donovans on the beach in St Kilda) and have a really nice night. We socialised a lot together. Cheryle referred to Graham as Pa—she loved him like a father. (He'd long had the nickname The Munster, because people reckoned he looked like Herman Munster.) I called him Pa, Pop and mostly Graham.

I went to Graham's house a lot—at one stage he lost his licence, so I picked him up and dropped him off a fair bit. I got to know his family well. Not many people went to Graham's house—he liked to keep his home life private (and I learned to be the same). We went to Graham's kids' weddings; in fact, the night his daughter was married at Rippon Lea, two blokes were arrested just up the road over the shooting of Michael Marshall. It made us wonder if we might have been the target.

Police used to think Graham's son (a locksmith) was involved in some of his jobs, but he wasn't. Graham never once asked his kids to be involved in anything in any way, shape or form. He wanted to keep them right away from all that.

Once, the police suggested that his son was implicated in a big robbery. The insinuation really upset Graham, because he'd worked so hard to give his kids a different life. (The police were always pretty keen on getting Graham—he was a bit of a trophy to them, but they never had much luck.) A lot of people want their kids to be the same as them, but Graham didn't. He was very strict—he made sure his children were educated and brought up the right way. And I followed him with that, and kept my kids away from all that nonsense. They all have jobs, are hard-working and are doing well. I'm proud of them. I never wanted them to be involved in the life I was.

Graham and I used to get about a bit, have a drink, muck around. He was great company. We went to the horse races now and then, until Graham was banned from the track in the late 1990s. He was quite devastated. He loved the races, especially mixing with different people there. And he was a good judge of a racehorse, had good information and had a lot of luck. He used to go to the races with only a little money, two or three grand, and his motto was that if luck was running his way, he'd hit it hard. He often turned that two or three grand into forty or sixty grand—and sometimes even one or two hundred grand.

Graham also came with us to the casino. He used to call me brain-dead, because I played the pokies. In the end, he was playing them himself. He loved them.

GRAHAM

Every now and then I'd eat with him at the exclusive Flower Drum restaurant. He ate there a lot—they even kept in the safe a pair of solid-gold chopsticks that belonged to him, and sometimes they brought them to his table on a red velvet cushion. Some people said he had a share in the business—I don't know if that was true.

Graham could mix with all types. He was a chameleon who could adapt to any situation and talk with anyone about any topic. And he was good at listening. If you had a problem, you could sit on a park bench and talk about it with him. You'd find a way through it—and what you said wouldn't go any further. I think that's why so many people respected him and gave him their confidence. He kept lots of people's secrets. And he's probably rolling over in his grave now, knowing I'm writing about him. He liked to stay under the radar.

A lot of square-heads who knew him sought his advice—even politicians and high-ranking police—and they knew his word was his bond. If he said 'This won't happen' or 'This will happen', then that was the outcome.

One day, Graham was having a meal at the Flower Drum with a dozen Painters and Dockers, when in walked TV and radio journalist Derryn Hinch. He had been broadcasting about how disgraceful the Painters and Dockers were.

Graham spotted him. 'Derryn, how are you?' he said. 'You know those Painters and Dockers you've been rubbishing on the TV? There's a few of them over here. Come and I'll introduce you.' And Graham dragged Hinch—who was trying to pull away from him—across to his table. Suddenly, Graham let go and Hinch went flying, knocking over a couple of tables.

Apparently, the next night Hinch appeared on his program, saying, 'I was in one of Melbourne's finer restaurants yesterday when I was accosted by a drunk'.

145

Another time, Graham was walking up the stairs to the restaurant when a gun fell out of his pocket, bounced off a few steps, and hit Hinch on the head, who was coming up the stairs behind him. A lot of people think that incident gave Hinch brain damage.

Graham loved animals, and one night driving home he spotted a ferret running across the freeway. He managed to catch it and took it home, naming it Patto after a mutual friend, Jeff Patterson. He loved the ferret and taught it some tricks.

Once, he had friends over and showed them how the ferret would give him a kiss. He held it up to his face, and the ferret grabbed hold of Graham's ear, bit it and wouldn't let go. Graham said it was like having a 10-pound earring. He had to put his head in the sink and his wife ran hot water on the animal before it would let go. The moment it released its grip, it sank its teeth into Graham's hand. He stopped doing ferret tricks for friends after that.

In November 2003, Graham came to see me and mentioned someone was going to try to kill him—he was on a 'hit list'. He laughed it off, saying he didn't believe it, but he was still on his toes.

He also warned me to be careful. 'Don't let anyone know what you're doing or where you're going', he said. 'But realise that if someone wants you bad enough they'll get you.'

I was more worried about him, so worried that I actually gave him a gun. He didn't want to take it, but I said it would make me feel better.

About the same time, Carl Williams sent a couple of blokes to see me. They came to say that Carl had no intentions of hurting Graham. (This was after I'd made it clear, earlier in the year, that Graham was off-limits.)

So, again, I sent a message back to Carl: 'Tell him, don't touch Graham'.

Graham was aware of Carl and his father, George—he wasn't friendly with them except to say 'Hello'. But Graham knew everyone. His views were the same as mine: Carl was an insignificant idiot, but he was dangerous because he'd made a lot of money from drugs, and he had these killers hanging around him looking for work. They were using their own product, becoming paranoid. It just needed someone to plant a seed in Carl's brain, and something stupid would happen. Graham knew that. He always said, 'Mick, they'll come unstuck and they'll fall on their own swords'. And he was right. But unfortunately Graham finished up as collateral damage.

19

HUNTING A KILLER

It was a Friday night in December 2003, and I'd got in late. About 2 a.m., the phone rang. Cheryle handed it to me—it was Lewis Moran. 'They've just killed Graham', he said.

'What?'

'They've just killed Graham.'

I couldn't believe it. I hung up and rang Graham's home. His wife, Sybil, answered.

'Don't tell me it's true', I said.

'Yes, it is—they've killed him.'

I quickly showered and drove to Graham's house. There were police everywhere. I went into his home and sat with his family. Like them, I was devastated, couldn't believe it.

It really shook me. Graham was very astute; he didn't miss much. He was aware of his surroundings, always looking in the mirror. It couldn't have been easy to get him. But they had.

Graham had been out for dinner, then picked up some things at the supermarket on the way home. They were obviously watching him and knew when he was coming home, because they were waiting. They were probably working with walkie-talkies. They got him as he was going to his front door. There were two getaway cars, one found burned out. It was a well-planned execution.

Graham had a gun, and I believe he let off a shot. Rumour has it—I don't know if it's true or not—that he shot the bloke in the shoulder. I'm spewing he didn't hit him between the eyes.

The funeral was a very sad occasion. People came from all over Australia, and the church was packed. I was a pallbearer. I remember the day vividly. I didn't see anyone from Carl Williams' team there, including Andrew Veniamin—they probably would have been torn to pieces.

Afterwards, as we talked quietly at his wake, everyone agreed that it was likely that Carl was behind it. There were other rumours, but the gut feeling was that it was Carl. I was filthy, like a caged lion. And I was determined to find out who had done it.

Until 13 December 2003, I had been just rolling along, doing my own thing. Different people were being killed—it was half-expected in some cases—and it had nothing to do with me. It was a fight about drugs. Whatever their issues were, it was their problem. Mind you, I was still careful. After the meeting between The Mediterranean and the boys from Perth went wrong, there was that word of a contract on my life. So I'd stepped up my protection.

In some ways it reminded me of the late 1970s, when there was a gang war in Melbourne that took several lives. One of those deeply involved was Brian Kane [*who ultimately became a victim*]. And I remember—I was only a teenager—he asked me: 'Whose side are you on?'

'Brian, I'm on no one's side', I said. 'This is not my fight.' And that was how I'd felt throughout the killings of 2003.

But once Graham was killed, everything changed. Whoever got Graham knew I might retaliate, so I was a threat—which meant I was the next likely target. I told my family to be very careful. I always telephoned before I went into the house, to make sure everything was all right. We had a codeword in case there was a problem. Les Kane had been killed by people waiting in his home, while his family were held at gunpoint. It's not hard to do—using stolen police uniforms would be just one way to make it more believable.

I heard again from different sources—a couple of ex-coppers, couple of current coppers—that there was a contract on my life. At one stage, detectives from the Purana taskforce came to see me, and offered protection for me and my family. I said no. I just wouldn't use it. I'm from a different school—we look after ourselves. To make it harder for anyone to get me, I mixed up my routine and movements, and told very few people my plans. I still felt comfortable at La Porcella (someone was usually loaded up there), and I believed the place was under surveillance. I thought I was as safe there as anywhere else. I carried a gun a lot, but it got to the point where I couldn't, because I ran the risk of being searched by police and charged—they had a fair idea what was going on. So there was always someone close to me who had a gun. If something was going to happen, it wasn't going to be easy for them. One of those who was loaded up was Ron Bongetti, who was in his mid-seventies. We spent a lot of time together, and he wouldn't have hesitated to use a gun if someone had a crack.

Late one night in 2003, Ron called me on the phone. It was about 3 a.m. 'Come and see me, now, please.' So I drove to Carlton to see him, and asked him what was wrong. Ron explained that he'd gone for his regular late-night walk. (He was ill and often couldn't sleep, so would go for a stroll.) He had been walking through the streets of Carlton when a carload of young blokes pulled up. They jumped out, walked up and demanded Ron hand over his wallet, threatening to harm him if he didn't. 'So I pulled my gun out and let a few shots go', Ron said.

He didn't aim for the young blokes, but apparently put a couple into the back of their car. He could have connected if he'd wanted to, but he just wanted to give them a fright. Ron said they ran like rabbits. Pretty funny, really, and it probably cured them of doing it again, which was a community service. The shooting was never reported to the police.

Not long after Graham was shot, I met Andrew Veniamin at La Porcella. We went for a walk.

'I think Carl's involved', I said.

Andrew denied it. 'Mate, it was nothing to do with us.' And he tried hard to convince me it wasn't Carl. But deep in my heart I knew it was Carl. I told Andrew I wanted to meet Carl in Carlton. Andrew made some inquiries, but Carl refused—he never had much dash in him—and would only meet at Crown Casino. Nowhere else. (There were countless surveillance cameras there. Nothing was going to happen in front of them.) So the casino it was.

Three days before Christmas in 2003, we met. Carl came with Andrew, and had a couple of his crew watching from close by. I went with Mario Condello, Ronnie Bongetti, Steve Kaya and a bloke called Farouk. (Steve and Farouk had first introduced me to Andrew.) They were all there because if I had a problem, they had a problem, and vice versa. That was the way we were. We didn't interfere with anyone—but if anyone interfered with us, we dealt with it.

The cameras filmed the meeting, and later the police employed lip-readers to decipher our conversation. The footage has also been shown widely on television—people often comment on how big I was. (I was over 140 kilograms then, wearing a big orange shirt that made me look like Demis Roussos [*a Greek singer who has battled obesity*] in a kaftan!)

I got straight to the point, and Carl strenuously denied any involvement in Graham's murder. He said he'd heard a strong rumour that Graham was killed after a deal with some Chinese went wrong. Apparently, someone owed this Chinese bloke a heap of money and Graham brokered a deal to get it back. He collected the money to give to the Chinese, but didn't hand it over. So the Chinese went to Graham's house to meet him and collect the money, an argument broke out and they killed him.

I knew it was just all bullshit, especially as Graham never invited people to his house. In fact, few people even knew where he lived. I dismissed that story right away.

'I heard he was a really good bloke', Carl said. 'Mick, I wouldn't have interfered with him.'

'You sent a message saying you wouldn't interfere with him, and the next minute he's dead', I said. 'I can't help but think you had something to do with it.'

'No, mate, I was out with the boys and we got drunk. You can ask them—they'll give me an alibi.'

'It mightn't have been you, but it was someone within your group', I said.

'Mick, I swear to you, I didn't do it.'

I told him I had nothing to do with the drug scene—I wanted to be left out of any problems there. 'The only involvement I've got is over who killed Graham', I said.

'Look, Mick,' he said, 'I've got no problem with you or any of your mates. Let's just leave it at that. I won't interfere with you, and please don't interfere with me'.

I wanted to make the situation clear. 'Mate, if you have a crack at one of us, we're going to come after you, as simple as that.'

He gave me his word nothing would happen. I didn't trust him as far as I could kick him. I still suspected Carl was behind it, but I wasn't 100 per cent sure—I had no proof. There were rumours and innuendos, which created some doubt. And you can't act on rumours.

I also wanted to know what Andrew had been doing the night Graham was shot. I was making active inquiries everywhere. I found out that Andrew had been at a place in Sunshine that night, with half-a-dozen people. Two who were there told me Andrew was very jumpy, on his toes. About 9 p.m., he received a call, and ran out of the place. The police also put him in Sunshine three hours later, when Graham was killed; in fact, they went to great lengths to insist he didn't do it (as part of the case to convict me of Andrew's murder). They put him there because his mobile phone was activated, and if you use a particular network it can trace you to a location. But it wouldn't have been hard for Andrew to leave his phone with someone. He was up to speed with all the police surveillance methodology, and knew how it worked. [*Police relied heavily on electronic surveillance, and in the two years before Veniamin's death he was stopped by police only three times, according to police evidence given at Gatto's trial.*]

I believe now that Andrew was part of Graham's murder and he knew it was going down. But I don't think he was at the scene, and I don't think he pulled the trigger.

I've since discovered the real reason that Graham was killed: paranoia. Whoever was consulting Carl told him that Graham was shopping around in Sydney for a hit man to kill him, on Lewis Moran's behalf. The story wasn't true, and Graham copped it for nothing. But those little killers, using their own product, fed this idea to Carl, telling him to kill Graham before he made a move. And I've got my suspicions about who the shooter was that night—but I have no proof. The only thing I'm certain of is that Carl Williams was behind it.

20

NO COMMENT

It was 4.04 p.m. on Tuesday 23 March 2004—less than ninety minutes after the shooting of Andrew Veniamin—and I was sitting in an interview room at Melbourne's St Kilda Road Police Station. I still couldn't believe what had happened.

I'd spoken to Cheryle again and talked to a lawyer, Zarah Garde-Wilson (more on her later). Within fifteen minutes of arriving, a forensics expert wearing yellow rubber gloves had swabbed my hands and face for gunpowder residue. (There wasn't any, probably because I'd washed after the shooting.) Then they took my clothes for testing, and I wore a jumpsuit for a while, until Cheryle sent in some spare clothes. I was given coffee and food and spoke to my main solicitor, George Defteros. At about 9.30 p.m., a doctor came and took a swab from my mouth for DNA, using a stick like a cross between a flat plastic spoon and a large ear bud.

At just after 11 p.m., more than eight hours after the shooting, the official interview began. Nine out of ten people in my position would have made a statement and explained what had happened. But I didn't. Over the years, I've learned that if you make a statement, you are locked into it. If you try to change your story—say, if something comes back to you—it can spell trouble. The police work on those changes, and when it comes to the trial they set you up. It's to *their* advantage if you make a statement. So the golden rule was—and still is—say 'No comment'. That was also my legal advice from George. So the interview took only a few minutes, because I wasn't prepared to answer police questions apart from saying, 'I've done nothing wrong. I've acted in complete self-defence. And I'd like to make no further comment at this stage'.

With that, I was charged with Andrew Veniamin's murder and locked up.

Going back to jail was nothing like in 1982. In those days, I mixed with other prisoners, ran to keep fit, had contact visits and countless phone calls, and pretty much ate and drank what I wanted, when I wanted. Twenty-two years later it was a completely different ball game.

Very quickly I was transferred to Victoria's largest jail, Port Phillip Prison, and put into a secure unit called Charlotte. I was kept in a cell, by myself, for twenty-three hours a day and allowed one hour of exercise, alone, in a small caged outdoor area. I was not allowed any direct contact with another prisoner. There were no contact visits, even with close family. Phone calls were limited, and the food was generally horrible. Whenever I left my cell to, say, go to the doctor (which was very rare), I was handcuffed and shackled, and the rest of the joint was shut down.

It was from one extreme to another. My life had been incredibly busy, involving family, friends, constant meetings, conversations, restaurant meals and endless phone calls (my phone never stopped). From that, I went to a cell by myself, with virtually no human contact.

In the first days I had panic attacks. I managed to talk myself out of them. 'Mate, relax, it's all in your brain', I'd say to myself as I felt an attack coming on. After a while they stopped. The brain's a pretty powerful tool.

Three or fours days after I arrived, I was walking to the yard for my hour's exercise when someone yelled out, 'Mick, is that you?'

'Yes', I said.

'Pick the newspaper up under the door.'

I spied the *Herald Sun* under the door of another prisoner's cell, so I grabbed it, walked out into the exercise yard and started reading. Inside there was a letter:

> My name is [*a killer in the Gangland Wars, whose name cannot be used for legal reasons*]. I was part of a surveillance team that was hired by Carl Williams and The Mediterranean to have you killed. Me and [*two others*] were paid to sit off your house, follow you, watch your movements and try and kill you.

He went on to explain that The Mediterranean had put up $400 000 to have me killed, but the hit team, hired by Carl Williams, had been offered only $200 000. Carl had obviously planned to keep a healthy commission. He said the hit team hadn't gone ahead because a couple of the would-be killers knew me, and had pulled the plug. They told Carl I was never home.

I didn't believe the letter-writer, so I sent back a letter the next day. 'Describe my house in Doncaster, exactly', I wrote.

The following day I picked up another note and he described my home to the letter: where the cameras were fitted, the slope of the hill, the layout of the street. He was telling the truth. In fact, he later signed an affidavit for my lawyers, telling them all about the plan to murder me. This bloke had already rolled and become a police informer. My lawyers thought the affidavit might be useful when my trial came up, but in the end we didn't use it.

In the days following the shooting, Cheryle and the kids stayed with my brother, John. I was helpless. I could do nothing. I kept in touch by phone every day. (I was allowed twenty-five phone calls each week, so had to limit myself.)

There was a newspaper report that my family had fled interstate, but it wasn't true. Apart from going to Cairns for a week's holiday, they were always about. My kids stopped going out much—they were pretty worried. It was traumatic all round.

A bit later, Andrew Allen, a copper from the Purana taskforce, came to see me. He was not a bad bloke.

'Could you please do me a favour, Andrew?' I asked him. 'Keep an eye on my family. If you don't mind, send a patrol car past the house every now and then.'

He said he'd arrange it. He also said, 'Mick, we've had calls to the police saying there's a drug laboratory running at your address in Doncaster. We know it's not true'.

The calls came from those rats who wanted to cause trouble by having police raid my house. There was all sorts of skulduggery going on. Thankfully, the police were awake to it.

NO COMMENT

Eight days after Andrew Veniamin was shot dead, he was buried. And, that night, they got Lewis Moran. I found out when one of the screws at the front desk buzzed me. (There was a buzzer in each room.) 'Look, I got some bad news for you', he said. 'They just killed Lewis.'

In some ways I was stunned. To kill Lewis was like running into a nursing home and killing a resident. The man was riddled with arthritis. He couldn't close his hands properly to grab a beer, let alone pull a trigger to save his life. In another way, it had been coming. Everyone knew Lewis was a target following the deaths of Mark and Jason. Detectives in the Purana taskforce had a whiteboard in their office with a list of possible targets: they were predicting who might go next. And Lewis was right near the top. It would have been nothing for them to have put surveillance on him and catch any killers in the act—and maybe even save Lewis' life. But it seemed they weren't interested in doing that, because it was 'only criminals killing criminals'. I reckon some police felt they could sit back and let it go.

For me, sitting in my tiny cell, it was deeply worrying. I was help-less, and feared even more for my family. I got a message to Cheryle to move out of the house, which she did. The rules had been thrown out of the window when Jason was gunned down in front of all those children—I realised anything was possible. Every hour as I sat in my cell, I listened to the radio, hanging on every bit of news.

I also held grave fears for several friends, with Mario Condello near the top of that list. And I was right. It turned out Carl wanted to kill Mario, and Mario knew it. It was just a matter of time before something happened—although the next victim was somewhat unexpected.

I had met Lewis Caine after he was released from jail in 2000. [*Caine had served ten years for murder.*] He was introduced to me by George Defteros, who told me Caine was a very willing bloke. Caine used to see me often, looking for work, driving me mad in the same way Andrew Veniamin did. 'Can you put me into something?' he'd say. 'I want to earn some big money.'

'Mate, I'm in the building business. Do you want a job on a building site?'

He was broke much of the time. Like Andrew, I gave him some money a couple of times. He would strut around with a bad attitude, like he had a chip on his shoulder. Some people called him a bantam rooster because of his jail walk and jail attitude. If anyone looked at him he'd be ready to go at any second.

He always treated me with respect and I thought he wasn't a bad bloke. But I'm not the greatest judge of character, and often take people too much at face value. And you can never judge a book by its cover—you never know what a man has deep in his heart. I liked Caine, and I felt a bit sorry for him. But I didn't realise, towards the end, that he had become very close to Carl Williams.

[*On 8 May 2004, Lewis Caine's body was found in an inner-city alleyway with a bullet to the head. Not long afterwards, two men, who we will call The Veteran and The Boxer for legal reasons, were arrested and charged. Both were later convicted and sentenced to long jail terms.*] My understanding is that Carl gave Caine $50 000 upfront to kill Mario. Caine went and saw The Boxer and The Veteran to get them involved, and The Veteran decided, 'Fuck it, let's just kill him and keep the money'. The Veteran was a low-life. I'm pretty sure that The Veteran was the one who shot him. He developed this strategy to say The Boxer did it, trying to bamboozle the jury, and create enough doubt to get it thrown out. It didn't work.

There were suggestions that Mario had found out about the plot and recruited The Veteran and The Boxer to kill Caine, but that's just bullshit. Mario had nothing to do with them in any way, shape or form. He knew better than anyone what sort of character The Veteran was. He couldn't be trusted to go and buy a bottle of milk. Everybody knew that. The only people that fell in with The Veteran were junkies and low-lifes that spent half their lives in jail. He was a great manipulator and a very ordinary bloke. Mario definitely had nothing to do with him.

It become apparent after Caine's death that I had a new problem. It turned out that Caine's girlfriend was Zarah Garde-Wilson, the solicitor who worked for George Defteros and advised me soon after I shot Andrew. A close friend of mine had visited the legal practice and had seen Caine, The Veteran and The Boxer all wandering around the offices. He was suspicious. No wonder.

Zarah Garde-Wilson worked in the firm that was preparing my legal defence. I don't like her. She knows that and knows why too.

The killing of Lewis Caine may have prevented an attempt on Mario's life. But Mario's problems were far from over.

21

REVENGE

Mario Condello knew the threat to his life was real. He believed Carl Williams wanted him dead, and had put out a contract. So Mario took precautions, including moving to the city. Mario wasn't going to be an easy target.

Early on the morning of 9 June 2004 a newsflash came on the radio that there'd been an attempted shooting in Brighton, and the gunmen had been caught. I knew straightaway it was Mario. When I got out of my cell at about 10 a.m., I rang a couple of friends and my family—they'd heard nothing, but quickly checked and found out I was right. They couldn't believe I knew before them.

[*That morning, as two men prepared to ambush and kill Mario Condello near Brighton Cemetery, in Melbourne's southern suburbs, the target himself was miles away. Police had the pair under surveillance, having stumbled onto the plot by accident when they bugged the car of a suspected drug dealer. As the two gunmen discussed whether a man walking his dog was their target, police pounced. Both gunmen, Sean Sonnet and a man who cannot be named for legal reasons, were later convicted and received lengthy jail sentences. At about the same time as* *the gunmen were grabbed, Carl Williams was arrested and also charged with conspiracy to murder Condello. He later pleaded guilty to the conspiracy, in which the gunmen were to be paid about $140 000. It was Williams' last day of freedom.*]

The trial prosecutor later claimed that Carl wanted Mario dead in revenge for Andrew Veniamin. I don't believe that was the main reason—Carl and Andrew had once been good mates, but there was no great love there when Andrew died. Carl had already started to distance himself from Andrew, although he used him for his own purposes. I think the motive was simply paranoia, the same reason they killed Graham. They tried to kill Mario because he was a danger. Carl thought Mario was the 'money man', and would be able to readily find the money to take out a contract to kill Carl. He was probably right too.

If Carl had succeeded, he would have just kept going. His team would have worked their way through my close friends, killing them all. They wouldn't have stopped.

Mario was worried about it, and sent his family overseas. I was worried too, thinking, 'Who's going to be next? Will they target my family?' It churned through my mind.

Eight days after Carl was arrested for conspiring to kill Mario, Mario was arrested for conspiring to kill Carl, his father and a third man. I have no doubt that Mario wanted Carl and his father killed. He probably thought, 'First in, best dressed'. After all, they were trying to kill him. But Mario had a problem with a rat. [*The rat was identified in court only as '166', which we will call him here, as he cannot be named for legal reasons.*] Charged alongside Mario, with conspiracy to commit murder and incitement to murder, was George Defteros— my solicitor!

[*That day, 17 June 2004, Condello and Defteros appeared in the Melbourne Magistrates Court. Police told the court that Defteros had contracted a registered police informer to carry out the killings. 'He alleged he had been approached by the defendant Defteros ... that there was work for him on behalf of Condello and they needed people they could trust', a detective told the court. He said the informer later wore an electronic wire in separate meetings with Defteros and Condello. 'During those meetings the informer was given the job to kill Carl Williams and George Williams and people that were described as minders', he said. During the meetings, details discussed included the Williamses' movements, a proposed getaway route, obtaining a false passport and disguises to be used. 'The arrangement was the informant was to receive $150000 per head, that's per killing', the detective said. Condello allegedly told the informer he wanted George Williams killed first.*]

Mario was remanded in custody. He was extremely confident that he'd beat it at trial. George was released on bail. [*Defteros claimed that he was totally innocent of the allegations. Fourteen months later, all charges against him were dropped when the director of public prosecutions said an analysis of the evidence led him to believe the trial should be discontinued.*]

George and I had a long history—he'd been my lawyer for many, many years. I really loved the man; he was behind us all the way. But when he was charged, he dropped me like a hot potato. He instructed his office not to talk to me. I used to ring—and he was my lawyer— and his office would say, 'George has given us strict instructions: we can't talk to you'. Up to that point, his office had been working on my defence, so I had to go elsewhere.

I'd paid George $40000 upfront, and he'd done next to no work. I tried to get the money back, but in the end told him to forget about it. There are not too many people who put money in a trust account and get any change, and George had shown me what he thought of me. In fact, he'd been demanding $200 000 upfront, and I was glad we hadn't paid that. He was continually bickering about money.

I also found out what George had been saying behind my back when I listened to the conversations he'd had with that slime-bag 166. Mario had access to the tapes in jail, so I listened to them, too. George said all sorts of things against me. At one point he told 166, 'I don't know how Mick's going to beat this; he had a body bag in the boot, for God's sake. He's going to do twenty years'. And this was my lawyer!

Our friendship ended. When someone finishes in trouble or in jail, that's when you really see what the person's made of. And he showed his true colours. I've seen him since and said 'Hello', but he is no longer a friend.

My cell was a tiny room, about 2.5 by 1.5 metres. It had a small shower and a toilet. (Imagine being locked in your bathroom for twenty-three hours a day and you'll get the idea.) I spent a lot of time reading legal documents ahead of my trial. I got the daily papers (which I paid for from my weekly prison spend). I had a television (a privilege that the screws could take away if a prisoner played up) and a radio. I always went with the flow, and the screws were pretty good to me.

To fill the time, I wrote letters. (Friends sent in books and magazines, but I wasn't allowed to have them.) And I received thirty or forty letters a week, sometimes more. The screws couldn't believe it. Those people who counted stuck with me—they will be friends of mine for life. Some of the mail I received was inspirational, such as a couple of pictures sent by 'Aussie' Joe Bugner. Those pictures now hang at home, with the words he wrote: 'Mick, when the going gets tough, the tough get going', and, 'Mick, Ali was tougher than he looked, trust me'.

Some people didn't bother contacting me, or writing. Some had already written me off—as far as they were concerned I would be doing twenty years. And when I got out I was pretty hard on a few of them, particularly the people I thought should have stuck with me. If I'd been found guilty and given a twenty-year sentence, it would have been interesting to see who would have stuck with me then. People forget about you very quickly when you're locked up.

I knew from day dot that I'd be all right; it was just a matter of going through the formalities. But I didn't think I'd be locked up for so long, and in such terrible, prehistoric conditions. Every six weeks I was moved to another identical cell—they wouldn't leave you in the same cell as a security measure. I would sometimes look through the hole in the door to see what was going on. There were prisoners being bashed by screws, people screaming and crying because they couldn't handle it. It was just unbelievable.

I had only one visit a week, which lasted one hour. I was separated from the visitor by a Perspex screen and couldn't touch whoever was there. Each visitor's name had to be on a list, or they couldn't see you. Sometimes I forgot to put a name down, so that person wouldn't be allowed to visit. All my visitors were searched, frisked and checked by a dog before they could get in. It was tough.

I soon got sick of television and letter-writing all day long, so I began an exercise regime. I did countless sit-ups and push-ups. I shadow-boxed in my cell for hours on end, like Hurricane Carter. [*Rubin*

REVENGE

'Hurricane' Carter was a boxer jailed for three murders in 1966. The question of his guilt was raised many times and featured in a Bob Dylan song. He was released after twenty years and his story was told in a film featuring Denzel Washington.]

Once I got out into the exercise yard I did chin-ups, jogged and worked out on the punch bag. I really punished that bag. The guards came over to watch because the whole joint shook when I hit that bag—I put a lot of force into it. One day I punched a hole straight through it. Over the fourteen months I spent inside, I became as fit as I'd been in years—and I shed 30 kilograms.

In December 2004, after a two-week hearing, I was committed to stand trial. The only good thing about my committal was that I got to see my family. I couldn't touch them, but I was excited just to be in the same room and spend the day with them.

One of those who stuck closest by me was my friend Michael, the businessman. He raised money for my court case and ensured that it was spent the right way. Michael is like a brother to me, and I can never thank him enough. People from all over Australia put money in for my legal defence, which cost about $680 000. I have since paid a lot of them back. Michael established a trust account and made sure that every bill was bona fide before it was paid. People used to drive him mad, wanting to borrow money for a few days, and he knocked them all back. He fell out with George Defteros, who wanted a massive upfront payment for legal work. Michael said, 'You do the work; I'll pay you'. Once George was charged, I had to find new lawyers.

For the new lawyers, too, a lot of my trial seemed to be about money. They were unbelievable. Once, we were told we were $300000 behind, which we challenged—it was nonsense. A week later, they said they'd had problems with the computer system, and we were right.

I used to ring the lawyer from jail. As the trial got nearer, I'd ring at least once a day to check how things were going. 'Mick, good to hear from you. Everything's going all right.' We might have a chat—I was really calling for moral support—and then he'd call someone to let them know I'd rung. They charged $500 for each call. That's how the bill blew out of proportion. Even during my trial, during the breaks, they wanted to discuss their fees rather than the case. On the day the jury went out to consider its verdict, one of the lawyers handed me a manila folder and said, 'You may want to have a look at this'. I opened it, and it was the latest bill. Sensitive timing. I told him to stick it up his arse.

I have to say that my barrister, Robert Richter, was entitled to every penny he charged, and probably more—he did a lot of work for me that I wasn't billed for. He really had the interest of his client at heart.

We found out that some people raised money for my defence—and kept it. One bloke in Melbourne raised more than $50000, and there were other people doing it too. So-called friends of mine were running around Sydney getting money, which they kept and spent. You can't forget things like that. It's a low act.

At the same time, there were those who were tremendous friends. One, Mario Amenta, took a $30000 cheque to George Defteros' office the day after I was charged, to ensure my initial representation. It was beautiful form, and a gesture I won't forget.

After some months in jail, I applied for bail. To get it we needed to show 'exceptional circumstances', and one of those was the conditions I was kept in—twenty-three hours a day locked up. Before my hearing came up, funnily enough I was shipped to another prison—Barwon—where I was also kept in high security, but allowed out of my cell for three or four hours a day. I didn't get bail.

My phone calls were still limited, but some were productive. In 2003, I'd put a fair bit of money on Makybe Diva, who won her first Melbourne Cup. She was racing in the Cup again in 2004, and I managed to make a couple of calls and back her pretty well again. She came home, which was fantastic. She ran again in 2005, and although she was not fancied and drifted in the betting, I went for it. And again, she won.

Most days I jogged for a couple of hours to keep fit. But I also got to mix with other prisoners, which was a bonus. (Previously, my interactions had been brief.) I once saw Andrew Fraser running around an enclosed yard, and had a chat with him for a couple of minutes. The screws weren't too happy. [*Fraser was a prominent criminal lawyer who was convicted of cocaine trafficking. He has since become a successful author and media figure.*] Another time a bloke yelled out at me through the fence. It turned out he was a cousin who I didn't know existed. (He was doing twenty years, and I still keep in touch with him by phone every week.)

For about six weeks, Mario Condello was there, before he succeeded in getting bail. (When Mario first applied for bail, Carl Williams wrote a letter that was given to the judge, saying, 'If you release Mario Condello on bail I hold grave fears for my father'. And they knocked Mario back.)

I also spent time with The Boxer. He was the man who had been meant to empty a machine gun into me from the back of a motorbike with Nik Radev, but the contract hadn't gone through because The

Mediterranean wouldn't pay an upfront fee. Radev had put a lot of pressure on, and The Boxer ended up in hospital having a nervous breakdown. He didn't want to do it because he liked me. I knew The Boxer from the fights and I didn't mind him. He was always respectful. Unfortunately, he was just led up the garden path by those evil rats. He was also caught up with The Veteran and had been involved in killing Lewis Caine. [*The Veteran and The Boxer were in Barwon Prison charged with Caine's murder.*]

The Veteran has always had a pretty big reputation. He never hesitated to shoot people—he once shot a policeman in the back. One night some years earlier, he'd been released from jail and had a drink with us in Lygon Street. I had a few drinks and left. A while later, the owner of the joint rang to say there were two blokes punching on out the front—it was The Veteran and his brother. I thought, 'What sort of animals are these blokes?' He was a dangerous low-life.

[*The Boxer and The Veteran were involved in one of the other Gangland Wars killings, which we won't identify for legal reasons.*] I kept asking about the murder and they kept denying it. They came to my cell door and knocked, and we'd talk through the door.

'Mate, you didn't kill him, did you?' I asked The Veteran.

'No, it wasn't me.'

'Your father would be rolling around in his grave if you did. He was a good mate of his; they grew up together.'

'I know. He has been a friend of the family for years. I wouldn't do that, mate; it wasn't me.'

He kept denying it. But it was both of them.

A few months later, The Veteran went missing a couple of times.

'Where's he gone?' I asked The Boxer.

'He's gone into hospital.'

I wasn't convinced. 'No, he's gone somewhere else; he hasn't gone to hospital.'

It turned out that he was doing a re-enactment of one of the gangland killings.

'I thought you told me you didn't do it?' I said when I saw him next.

'I didn't', he said.

'Well, how could you be doing a re-enactment?'

'I'm just doing it because if they charge me, I can prove that it wasn't right.' It was bullshit.

[*The Boxer and The Veteran were later charged with this murder and convicted. The Veteran became an informer, providing details on the Gangland Wars to Purana taskforce detectives.*]

My trial was set for May 2005. Shortly before it began, I asked for a leave pass to see Ron Bongetti, who was very ill in hospital with terminal cancer. I told the authorities he was like a second father. It was a plea for a last visit.

One morning they came and got me from my cell. Because it was a high-security prison, they never gave you any warning about what you were going to do.

'Come on, we're going', the screws said.

'Where are we going?'

'We'll tell you when we get there.'

They shackled me up and walked me through the jail. I was about to be put in the back of the van when I said, 'Where are you taking me? I want to know before I get in that van. I want to know'.

'We're taking you to the hospital.'

'Oh, beautiful.' I was going to see Ron.

'No, we're taking you to the Eye and Ear Hospital to have your eyes checked.'

I was devastated. 'I don't want to go.'

'Are you sure?'

'Thanks, I'm sure. Just take me back to my cell.'

They walked me back, and that was as close as I got to seeing Ron. He died on Anzac Day, 25 April, 2005. I thought he'd hang on, but he didn't pull through, the poor bugger.

They told me at 6 a.m. the next day. I was in shock; I couldn't believe it. It was only days before my trial was due to start, and Ron's death really unsettled me. I wasn't allowed to go to his funeral, either, to say goodbye. It was hard. He was a good man.

22

TRIAL BY JURY

Shortly before my trial for the murder of Andrew Veniamin began, the Crown prosecutor sent me a message, delivered by my barrister, Robert Richter. 'If you plead guilty to manslaughter, they guarantee you will do no more than six years' jail.'

I was pretty surprised.

'It's not a bad deal', said Richter. 'If you go down for murder, you're going to get twenty-five years. If you want to do a deal, we can nod our head for six years.'

I wasn't even tempted by the offer. I had a very strong case and I believed I'd be acquitted. I also knew I couldn't face six years in jail.

'We'll fight it all the way. Tell him to get fucked.'

My confidence had been given a boost two weeks after my arrest, when Purana taskforce police visited me in jail. They brought a letter from police chief commissioner Christine Nixon telling me I was banned, by her, from the Crown Casino for ten years. The letter had greatly lifted my spirits. I was facing twenty-five years' jail if convicted of murder, and this was a ten-year ban. 'They must think I'm going to beat it', I thought. (Some years later, when I organised a fundraiser for the 2009 Victorian bushfires, I spoke to Nixon's secretary, asking if Nixon would attend. And I said, 'While you ask her, can you thank her very much for barring me from the casino? She's done me the biggest favour of my life. I wanted to send her a diamond ring but I thought people might think I was trying to corrupt her'. She got quite a chuckle out of that.)

My main fear about the trial was that if a juror held out, it would be a mistrial. And, funnily enough, when they empanelled the jury, one member's mother was friendly with a Purana detective involved in the case. When the juror made it known, Richter said to me, 'We can abort, and go for a new jury. But I reckon they're pretty good, the ones we've got. My advice is run with it'. I was very hesitant, but went with Richter's advice, which turned out to be spot-on.

My daily routine for the trial was unpleasant. Each day started at about 5.30 a.m. with a shower, followed by breakfast at 6 a.m. I had to be ready by 6.30 a.m., when the screws collected me from my cell. They handcuffed me and took me to a holding area, where I swapped my prison clothes for a suit. My legs and feet were shackled, then they put a waistband on me—a big leather strap that went around my body, and was done up tightly. My handcuffs were bolted to the belt, so I couldn't move much. Then they helped me into the back of a 2-tonne van, with its windows blocked out, so it was completely dark inside. I always travelled alone. They drove me out of the prison with an escort car. I could hear the security guards load their guns before we left, in case someone tried to bust me out!

The trip from Barwon to the Supreme Court in the city took an hour and a half each way. I was pretty fit, so I didn't move around too much. At some stages of the journey I had to drag myself into the corner of the van and open my legs as far as I could—which was about 30 centimetres—so that I didn't go flying when we went round a corner. The security team were quite good blokes, and didn't drive badly on purpose. Nonetheless, I felt like a trussed crab in a stainless-steel box that someone shook now and then.

On arrival, the van would reverse round the back of the Supreme Court. When they opened the door it was beautiful—I could see daylight. I was taken to a tiny holding cell, where I paced and paced until it was time to go into court. Once I got into the courtroom, they took my shackles and handcuffs off. My family sat right behind me and I could talk to them, which meant the world to me.

On my first day, I wore clothes that had been blessed by a priest in Geelong. This was organised by Mat Tomas, my business partner, who had seen the priest with Cheryle, and told him all about me. The priest had blessed the suit, shirt, tie, socks, underwear, shoes— everything—and told them I'd be acquitted, but I had to wear these clothes on my first day in court.

The clothes were blessed on a Sunday, the day before my court hearing began. But prison rules meant that any new clothes had to go through a series of security checks, and there was no way I would have them in time. I made a special appeal to the head of the jail— I told him this was important to my family—and he pulled a few strings and managed to do it. I was very grateful.

The court process was a game. For the coppers, it was a game. For the prosecution, it was a game. And the aim of the game was to find me guilty.

The prosecutor involved in my committal and trial, Geoff Horgan, was as shifty as a shithouse rat—he used every trick in the book to make sure I was convicted. After I was committed to stand trial, just before Christmas 2004, I applied for bail. The prosecution produced a statement from an informer saying that a week before I shot Andrew Veniamin, I told this bloke I had a hit list, and that I would kill Andrew and then Carl Williams. It was absolute rubbish. And this informer was never produced at my committal or even my trial—this evidence wasn't presented, because it was rubbish. They even produced details of an investigation by the Australian Crime Commission, which supposedly investigated a number of people and their involvement in drug importations. Over three years of investigation, no charges were laid. It was all rubbish, but I didn't get bail.

When it came to my trial, the prosecution introduced a heap of material from secret hearings of the Australian Crime Commission. Or at least I thought they were secret, until they were brought up in open court. When I went to the hearings, about the time Jason Moran was killed in mid-2003, I was led to believe that anything I said would not see the light of day. I even thought my appearance itself was meant to be a secret. Not so. [*The Australian Crime Commission has the power to compel witnesses to answer questions. Its hearings are secret, and those called are not allowed to tell anyone, except their legal counsel, even that they have been called to give evidence. This very secretive organisation has restrictions on what can be published about its hearings. Had the documents not been given as evidence in court, these matters would not be raised in this book.*]

The central argument in my trial was not whether I killed Andrew Veniamin, but whether I had acted in self-defence. And the key to that was whether Andrew had arrived that day with a gun. [*By law, the prosecution did not have to prove a motive, although it hinted at Gatto seeking revenge for Graham Kinniburgh's murder and/or a belief that Gatto thought he might be Veniamin's next victim.*] Horgan summed it up when he told the jury: 'If you think that Veniamin had the gun, he was the one who had the gun as they walked into that back passageway, I can sit down now. Your verdict will be not guilty. It's a critical issue in this case'.

I had to explain that not only did Andrew arrive with the .38, but that I had my own gun, which I didn't use.

Five days after I was arrested, on 28 March 2004, Colin Lovitt, a senior criminal barrister, had come to see me in jail. (Lovitt is one of the few lawyers who genuinely has his client's interests at heart. He is a true fighter for the underdog.) I told him that I was carrying my own gun the day I shot Andrew—a small .25 handgun—in my pocket. But Andrew had moved so quickly that I hadn't had time to pull out my own gun—if I'd tried, I have no doubt I'd be dead. Instead, we wrestled with his gun and he died. But once Andrew was dead, I thought the .25 I was carrying was a problem, so I gave it to a friend at La Porcella, Brian Finn, and told him to take it. I knew the police were monitoring me and suspected the room was bugged, so I whispered in Lovitt's ear that I had a gun. 'Just keep that to yourself for now' was his advice. Brian left before the police arrived.

More than eight months later, the committal had begun. We raised our evidence about this gun, and the prosecutor, Geoff Horgan, jumped up and made a song and dance about it. He was quite mischievous about it, and continued this line through the trial. He said the second gun was 'a recent invention and a concoction'. He said if it was true, we would have screamed it from the rooftops long ago.

I was furious. Not only was it something that I had explained to my lawyers at the first opportunity after the shooting, but Horgan knew this. Lovitt had told him about our jail conversation, and said that for him to suggest the gun was a 'recent invention' would not be true. But Horgan kept pursuing the angle.

Lovitt was far from happy about it, and made a statement about our conversation. In fact, he was prepared to give evidence at my trial about it, but the Supreme Court judge Justice Cummins wouldn't allow it. He said, 'There'll be no lawyers giving evidence in this trial'. Apparently, Cummins and Lovitt had come to verbal blows in previous trials—Lovitt was very outspoken. The judge said that Lovitt could write a statement that would be shown to the jury, and that was it.

During the trial, the prosecution produced the tape of a phone call from me in jail to a friend, Steve Kaya, talking about 'Brian'. [*The phone had been bugged.*]

I said, 'Did you seen Brian?'

In reply, Steve said, 'I'm taking him away for the weekend, and we'll sort it out then'.

The prosecution used this as 'evidence', and implied that Steve was planning to take Brian Finn away for the weekend, and either put pressure on him or word him up on what evidence to give. It turned out that the conversation kept going—and I was talking about one of my lawyers called Brian, and complaining about how much he was charging me. In fact, the tape wasn't too complimentary. Richter got up and asked that the tape be played a bit further (which it was, but not in front of the jury). When the rest of the tape was played, that nonsense was put to rest.

The key to the prosecution case was that Andrew Veniamin did not have a gun when he arrived at La Porcella, and that I'd shot him in cold blood. They said the forensic evidence proved that, even after he was wounded, I kept firing. It was all nonsense, and Richter successfully explained this to the jury.

Richter contradicted a large part of the prosecution's forensic case and dismantled their arguments. He is very good with ballistics, firearms, blood splatter—he loves those sorts of cases. Some of the prosecution arguments were quite fanciful, and Richter put forward the principle of Ockam's Razor, which has been around since the 1300s. In short, it means that the simplest explanation is the most likely one. [*The theory states: 'Entities should not be multiplied unnecessarily'. The term 'razor' refers to the act of shaving away unnecessary assumptions to get to the simplest explanation. Thus, if two hypotheses are equally accurate and neither appears more probable than the other, the simple one is to be preferred over the complicated one, because simplicity is practical.*]

The prosecution said that there was no way Andrew could have carried a concealed gun because of the tight-fitting clothes he was wearing. They went to great lengths to point out that it was a heavy gun—the jury got to feel the weight of it—and said that if Andrew had walked around the restaurant, the gun would simply have fallen out.

I came up with an idea. I asked my lawyers to borrow a .38 revolver from a friend who owned a gun shop, find someone the same size and shape as Andrew Veniamin, put identical clothes on the model, and get him to walk around with the gun concealed in his clothes. He filmed the exercise—this bloke put the .38 behind his pants and walked around the room, sat down, stood up, and then lifted his jumper to show the gun. It was clear that Andrew could have easily carried the gun without anyone seeing it.

Richter somehow found a way of getting our re-enactment shown to the jury. So the prosecution decided they should do their own re-enactment—and they found a big, tall copper and put him in tight-fitting clothing, and when he walked around the gun kept hanging out. It was a complete joke compared with what actually happened. When the jury watched it they were laughing because it was so ridiculous.

Great friends like Steve Kaya and Farouk helped greatly during my trial in dismantling the prosecution's case. They went and found witnesses in Melbourne's western suburbs who had been attacked and shot by Andrew Veniamin, showing Andrew's habit of carrying a hidden gun. They talked these witnesses into making statements— which was against their principles—and the witnesses gave evidence in court. They never left a stone unturned. That's when you find out who your friends are—in bad times, not in good times—and Steve and Farouk came through for me.

I wanted to give evidence and tell the jury what had actually happened that day. But Richter advised me not to. 'Mick, I think you're a mile in front. I don't recommend that you give evidence yourself. The downside is they won't know what happened in that room, except that you both went out there and he was killed. The upside is you give evidence and all that comes out, but they're going to attack your credibility, attack you everywhere. They will keep you in the witness box for days and drive you mad.' He paused. 'It's your call. My advice is you don't do it.'

'I want to do it', I said.

'Are you sure?'

'Yes, I'm sure. It's important that it comes out what took place in that room.' The prosecution were claiming that I'd executed Andrew and shot him as he lay on the ground. 'Whatever they attack me with, I can handle myself.'

'Okay, it's your call', he said.

We decided that Mark Taft, Richter's junior counsel, should question me, which really freaked them out. Then Horgan, for the prosecution, got up and started attacking me. It was a nasty game. Even before I got into the box he was pointing at me, calling me a 'demonstrable liar'. I felt like jumping out of the box and clocking him. But I kept my cool and even managed to give him a little bit back when he cross-examined me. He didn't like it one bit. I was in the box for almost two days.

One piece of evidence the jury didn't hear was the fact that I'd had a body bag in the boot of my car, as well as a couple of bullets (which I suspect had fallen out of Ron's gun many weeks before the incident). The prosecution thought they had hit a goldmine—a body bag! But when the trial started, Justice Cummins ruled it as inadmissible for some reason. The Crown was very upset.

On paper it didn't look good. I realise not every bloke has a body bag in his boot, but it was no big deal to me. I could explain it in a heartbeat. It came from Mario Condello, who was heavily involved in a funeral parlour. It was in the boot of his car, and one day he gave it to me. 'Do you want this?' he asked.

'What is it?'

'It's a body bag.'

'What the fuck am I going to do with that?'

He suggested I use it for storage, so I took it. It sat in the boot of my car for months, and was still there when I was arrested. There was no motive or malice to having that body bag.

At lunchtime on 14 June 2005, the jury went out to consider their verdict. I was worried. I thought, 'What hope have I got of beating this?' I knew one of the jurors had links to the police. By evening they hadn't reached a decision, so I was returned to Barwon Prison.

The next morning, I was back at court, waiting. At lunchtime, after eight hours of deliberation, word came through that the jury had reached a decision. I was taken from my cell back into the court—and it was a completely different scene. Every day for all seven weeks of the trial, my family and friends had been sitting near me—we often had a chance to talk in the breaks. But this time I came into the court and only my wife and children were nearby. The rest of my family and my friends were in the upstairs gallery. The other seats were taken by reporters and police, including plenty from Purana. It made me think of when the Romans threw the Christians to the lions in large arenas. They were all looking for a bit of flesh and blood.

Justice Cummins told everyone in the court, 'Whatever the decision, whether it be guilty or not guilty, I expect you all to be nice and quiet. I don't want to hear any noise or disruptions'.

When the jury walked in to take their seats, they didn't look at me, and I had a bad feeling. They were all looking down. Normally when they walked in, a couple of them would look around—but not this time. They didn't look too happy. The foreman of the jury was a schoolteacher, and he stood up to give the jury's verdict.

'Not guilty.'

I'll never forget that moment. The courtroom was like the MCG—it erupted. There was clapping, cheering, yelling and screaming. It was just unbelievable. For me, it was like the world had been lifted off my shoulders. It was a great feeling. I was ecstatic. And two or three people on the jury were crying. It was quite an emotional moment.

When the noise settled down, the judge told me I was free to go. But instead, the security guards took me back upstairs. As I walked past Richter I gave him a kiss on the cheek, and shook the hands of a couple of lawyers and reporters. I was taken upstairs, where I was kept for about an hour, as they checked to see if I had any outstanding warrants. Once that was completed they let me go, and I walked outside into the street. A heap of people were waiting, and they just swamped me. It was great to hug my wife, my daughter and my sons for the first time in fourteen months. And it was all captured in front of television news crews, who recorded me saying, 'Thank God for the jury system, and thank God for Robert Richter'.

After a while we made our way to a car, jumped in and drove home—and people started flowing in. About a hundred people were there, and we ordered pizza, drinks—it was fabulous. I hadn't had a cigar or alcoholic drink for fourteen months. Food tasted great, and it was fantastic that I could grab people and give them a hug and kiss. *Herald Sun* photographer Peter Ward, who I've known for years through boxing, came back and took photos.

Despite the fact that I was innocent, I knew I was lucky to get through the trial. Once you become a target, and the director of public prosecutions, the police and the prosecutor are all working together to convict you, things can get tough. There was a lot of pressure for a conviction. I was the first of the gangland trials, and the police were desperate for a result. When I was acquitted, they were devastated.

23

BACK IN TOWN

The day after my release, I jumped in my car and drove off like nothing had changed. I took my briefcase and shot down to see my lawyer. At lunchtime, I had something to eat with the boys in Carlton. It was just a beautiful feeling being free, walking around. [*Gatto was snapped by a News Limited photographer in Lygon Street, and his first lunchtime meal was a feature in many papers.*]

I weighed 108 kilograms and I was very fit. I'd lost a lot of weight—some friends thought I was ill; others barely recognised me. Yet within two years I was back up to 140 kilograms. My weight still fluctuates—I can easily move up or down 20 kilograms. But I know one thing—I'd rather be fat and free than thin and inside.

While I was in jail I was always training hard, and I had one focus—getting out. That was all I thought about. I had to front the trial and, as far as I was concerned, I was going home. So when I came out I was ready, and quickly back to normal. But I was very much on my toes. My goals were simple: to stay free, protect my family and stay alive. I knew I was still a target, and people wanted to kill me. The Mediterranean still had a lot of money, a lot of power, a lot of police on his side, and a lot of crooks on his side. Many people I knew—acquaintances—had sided with him. People are like sheep: they follow the money. I fronted him and he denied he was planning to do me any harm. Then he had his own 'problems' and that was it. [*These 'problems' cannot be described for legal reasons.*]

One of the first things I did was show my thanks to Robert Richter. Days after my release I went to a tattooist in North Melbourne. Anyone who says having a tattoo doesn't hurt is a liar. Imagine twenty or thirty needles puncturing your skin, putting colours under the skin so they stay there forever. The punctures become a scar that scabs up—and when the scab goes, it ends up a colourful scar. It took a couple of hours—I now have 'Robert Richter', 'Not Guilty' and 'Ockam's Razor' tattooed on my chest.

Once the scars healed I went to see Robert in his office, and showed him.

He laughed. 'You're mad', he said. 'I hope you don't regret it.'

'How would I ever regret it?' I said. 'You're a beautiful man and I love you.'

It's true. Unlike many other lawyers, Robert is not a parasite who sees you as a dollar sign. He wants to win and do the right thing by his client, no matter who they are.

Soon after my release, police came to see me. They were concerned about my safety. I had no interest in police protection, and told them. Instead, they wanted to put cameras around my house.

'No', I said.

'Can we lock into your cameras that you've got at home?' they asked.

'No', I said.

But I spoke to my family about it; all of us sat down together. 'The police seem to think I'm the next target', I said. 'They want to access our cameras at home, get a live feed and watch it in the

Purana office. I don't want to do it, but I have to ask you how you feel about it.'

The family were all for it. 'You have to do it, Dad. Think about us', one of my kids said.

One thing led to another, and I let the police access the cameras. They had direct coverage of who was coming up and down the street, when I left, when I came home—they knew every move I made. This went on for about a year. In the end, they were forever sending technicians over to 'fine tune' things—God knows what they were up to. And I'd had enough, so asked them to stop. The whole place was probably monitored by then, but I treated it as if it was anyway. I'd done that all my life: it was the best policy. (If you act as if your home is bugged, you never have a problem.)

I asked them several times to take it all out. They wouldn't. 'If you don't come and pull it out by the end of the week, I'll get my blokes to pull it out', I said. They sent a team over right away, and took a box out of the roof.

Two weeks after my release, I went on radio, speaking to John Silvester [*aka Sly of the Underworld*], Ross Stevenson and John Burns on the 3AW breakfast program. It was my first planned media appearance since being released. A lot of journalists wanted to talk to me and had been calling my lawyers' office, wanting to do deals. Quite a few had come to my house, too. It was driving me mad.

'If there's a media outlet or a talkback show that's prepared to pay a six-figure sum that goes directly to the Royal Children's Hospital, I'd be more than happy to give my input and chat along those lines', I told the 3AW listeners. 'I'm not interested in doing it for the glory or the publicity, but if the price is right and it's a worthy cause, I'd be prepared to do it. Otherwise, I just want to be low-key and be left alone to do my own little thing, if I can.' The price wasn't right, and no one took up the offer. But most importantly it got the media off my back and they all went away.

Within days I was back at work with my business partner, Mat Tomas. I met Mat twenty years ago—he used to run around a lot with Alphonse. Mat's Croatian, loves soccer, and we became close friends about ten years ago.

Mat had been working at a crane company called TJF, which had gone bust. In fact, they ended up robbing the banks—$180 million went missing. I don't know exactly what happened, but the money disappeared and Mat was left without a job.

In mid-2003, some months after TJF collapsed, Mat came to see me and said, 'Are you interested in starting a crane company together?'

I said, 'I've got no real money to put in. How are we going to do it?'

He explained. When he had worked for TJF, he'd formed a good relationship with a crane company salesman, David. This bloke now worked for Grove, a massive international crane company, and they wanted a market share in Australia. David had rung Mat, and said the company would effectively underwrite up to $10 million of cranes. Was Mat interested?

I introduced Mat to a bloke that found the finance, and we were away. We borrowed the money from a bank, and paid off the interest every month. What made the deal possible was that Grove provided a buyback guarantee—if we failed in the first five years, Grove would buy back the cranes. In other words, the bank that lent the money had no risk. If the venture failed, one of the largest crane manufacturers in the world had guaranteed that the bank would get its money back.

We initially bought $8 million of cranes, and paid GST, which was refunded to us by the tax department. We used that money as working capital, which meant we could get the business up and running. We decided to paint the cranes black and call the company Elite Cranes.

At the start we had a bit of luck, and we managed to survive. While my building contacts helped, Mat's contacts were more important. He had been in the industry a long time and had a great network.

Our main problem was that soon after we started the business, I was arrested and charged over Andrew Veniamin's murder. The day of the shooting, we took the lease on our massive warehouse in Brooklyn. But Mat and my two sons, who both work at Elite (Damien is now general manager), managed to build a fantastic business. At the time of writing this book, we have twenty cranes and sixty employees. We've managed to turn it into a $20 million-a-year business (and we pay a fortune in tax), which we'll own in a few years. Both Mat and I draw a salary. And despite the recent tough economic times, we have some long-term contracts with blue-chip companies, which means Elite should survive, while others may go broke.

So when I came out of jail, in June 2005, I walked into a job and a booming business. I cannot thank Mat enough for what he did while I was away, and what he has done since. Elite is truly a great Australian company.

The taxman (whose name was Bernie) also paid me a visit once I was out. I had been subpoenaed to a couple of hearings that I can't talk about. [*The Australian Crime Commission has strict secrecy provisions, although a lot of information was used at the murder trial.*] In the end, Bernie told me I owed $1 million. It was a ridiculous figure. In short, they couldn't understand how my life worked. In simple terms, when I have money, I'm generous with it. I give it to people who need it. I've always been that way. And I spend a lot of time hanging around gamblers, who are often the same. One time, an old bloke called Sam, who started with $10000, won $5 million at the casino playing baccarat. He gave me money all the time: $50000, $80000, $100000, $200000. 'Don't worry about giving it back', he said. Gamblers are like that. If I'm gambling and I'm winning a lot of money, people line up—there's a queue of people. And I don't mind doing that. So when I was asked by the authorities to give them a list of people who lent me money, it was a long list, and the 'debt' ran into the millions. I 'owe' some people enormous amounts, and they've said, 'Don't worry about it'.

Bernie had left me alone while I was awaiting trial, but once I was out he came to see me. They thought I was living beyond my means and couldn't prove where the money came from.

'You have to fix up this tax problem, Mick', Bernie said.

'You're not getting a dollar', I said. 'Your statement is just all bullshit. I have no assets—there's nothing in my name. And I simply don't know how you arrived at that figure. The easiest thing for me to do is go bankrupt, and you'll get nothing.'

The house was in the kids' names (through a trust company). Bernie had done his homework on my 'assets' (I had nothing, anyway—I'd just got out of jail) and he knew I meant what I said. So we negotiated. In the end we settled on $200000, which I paid off in instalments. And that tidied up my tax problem.

24

MARIO

Mario Condello was confident he would beat the charges of conspiring to murder Carl Williams, Carl's father and one of Carl's minders. The same charges against George Defteros had been dropped, and Mario had a good grasp of the evidence (he was a trained lawyer).

On 6 February 2006, the evening before his trial was to begin, we had a couple of drinks at the Society Restaurant, in the city. We mucked around, had a talk—he was in pretty good form. I left at about 6.30 p.m., and he had a meal with his lawyer.

At about 10 p.m., Mario arrived home. He was on bail and his curfew was 10 p.m., although he rarely observed it—he often got in much later. They never enforced it that hard. He drove into the garage and went to close the garage door when someone confronted him. Mario was on the phone, talking to a woman. He said to her, 'Hang on a second'. The next minute she heard a few shots—and that was it.

Mario's son rang me. I was in Brunswick with a few of the boys. He told me his dad had been shot and killed. I just couldn't believe it. I went white. I'd thought all the killings were over. We jumped in the car and raced down there at 100 miles an hour. It was all cordoned off. The coppers wouldn't let us through so we left, and went and had a coffee, in shock, wondering who had done it.

The next day there was a team of journalists camped outside my home. Some were on my front lawn, some across the road with cameras. They were phoning me and knocking on the door.

'Leave me alone. I don't want to talk to you', I told them.

I was filthy. No one could walk out of the house without being photographed. They'd given out my address on television—now every hit man in Australia knew where I lived. So I walked out of the house in my dressing gown with a pocketful of eggs, and let some go. Three eggs, three bullseyes. I hit a camera and two cameramen. I was screaming, 'Fuck off! Leave me and my family alone. All you people are doing is getting people killed'. (Afterwards I was asked several times, 'Why did you throw eggs?' My reply: 'Because I'd run out of hand grenades'.) I was so angry I wasn't thinking straight. My mind wasn't right. At one point I was going to grab a baseball bat and smash some cameras. Then I was going to ring a few bikie mates and get a team of them to come. I'm glad I didn't. Commonsense prevailed.

In the end, a couple of journalists came to the door and said, 'Mick, we're only doing our job. Our bosses tell us to come here. We have to come—that's what we get paid to do'. They were right. 'If you can just come out, check your letterbox and say a few words, we'll go away and leave you alone.'

So I walked out to the letterbox in my dressing gown, they asked me a couple of questions, I walked back inside, and they packed up and left.

Mario was born in Calabria, and he loved the Italian way, the Calabrian way. He was more Calabrian than anyone I know. He was more Calabrian than the Calabrians in Calabria. He'd come over with his old set ways and he'd never changed.

Mario was a good friend; we were very close. He was smart and we did a lot of things together. He had a lot of charisma. I miss him.

People would come to us with problems and we'd solve them— money owed, business issues, troubles in the family, marriage problems, anything. We used to mediate for a fee. Mario was very smart at doing things in a legally correct way, so we complemented each other.

I spent a lot of time with Mario in the 1990s, going to his house for barbecues and functions. But his wife went a bit funny. She's a pretty educated woman and just didn't like what Mario had become involved in. She wanted him to live a 'normal life'.

Mario had studied in the same class as Gareth Evans, and could have been a politician, a prosecutor, a judge. But he liked the other life—the Mafia image, the gangster side of things. It was the way he was, unfortunately.

In the 1980s, Mario was charged with trying to extort money from a bank. I can't remember the details of the case, but it involved a copper who drove Mario mad. Mario went to court and he beat it—and this copper was furious. He really had it in for Mario, wanted him like he wanted a trophy on his wall.

One night in the mid-1990s, two blokes battered this copper at his home; they gave him a really good clip. And the rumour was the two blokes were both big; the descriptions fitted me and Mario.

A couple of coppers I knew came to see me. 'Mick, there's a taskforce being formed. They're going to come and get you and Mario—and be warned, they're probably going to shoot you.' They said twenty or thirty coppers would be out there looking for us—and they'd shoot on sight.

Mario and I were pretty worried, and we decided to see a friend who had a pizza shop in Footscray. We stayed in the refrigerated area for hours—it was freezing! As we sat there, I remembered I'd stored some rifles in Mario's office. We had to get rid of them. Mario wouldn't move, so I shot down to his office and gave them to a bloke I knew to get rid of. If I'd been arrested there and then, I would have been in plenty of bother.

I headed back to the pizza shop, and Mario was still there, very cold. He went to use his mobile and I jumped up and stopped him. 'The moment you press "Send", they'll know where we are.' He didn't make the call.

Early the next morning—we were almost snap-frozen—we went to a mate's house to thaw out, and got on the phone. We rang a lawyer and arranged to visit the St Kilda Road Police Station.

Not long after we arrived, a high-ranking copper came in and sat down. 'Mick, I've never had a problem with you. I've always liked you. I've always said to myself, "I'm never going to interfere with you unless you interfere with us". On this occasion, it's clear that you've interfered with us.'

'Mate, it wasn't us', I said. 'I assure you: it wasn't us.'

We weren't charged and, in the end, the police worked out who did it. It was a close call.

The conspiracy to murder charges, and particularly the time in jail on remand, had left Mario depressed. He'd found jail a lot tougher than it had been in the 1980s, when he'd breezed through. This time he came out quite sick, and after his release he spent some time at a psychiatric hospital in Richmond.

His funeral was big, and a very sad occasion. I gave a reading and helped carry the coffin from the church. Not long after the funeral, his wife moved away and changed her name.

No one has been charged with Mario's murder—nor has anyone been charged with Graham Kinniburgh's murder. It seems police have 'solved' most of the others, but not these two. Perhaps they don't worry about Graham and Mario as much.

I don't believe that Mario's death was gang-related, although someone took the opportunity to make it look like it was part of the Gangland Wars. I believe he was killed for other reasons. He'd made a few enemies over the years—handling people's money and other things—and I believe it may have been related to that. I believe, however, that Carl Williams had something to do with it. One rumour is that [*a criminal we can't name for legal reasons*] was paid by an Italian to do it, and that Carl helped put it together. Time will tell.

25

OUT OF THE SHADOWS

After Mario's murder I got stuck into work, keeping my head down, and trying to stay under the radar. I'd had enough publicity for a lifetime. The murder had thrown my name back into the spotlight, and I didn't like it. But in the three months that followed, things went quiet.

Then in June 2006, it all went crazy again. First, I was called to the Supreme Court to given evidence in an unfair dismissal case. It revolved around Ted Sent, who'd been sacked as chief executive of Primelife, a company listed on the stock exchange. He was suing for $5 million in lost earnings, and called me as a witness.

I had been introduced to Ted in the late 1980s or early 1990s by a bloke called Emilio Giannarelli—they were in partnership. Ted was a very entrepreneurial, smart man. He'd been bankrupt a couple of times and had bounced back. He was resilient and tenacious. When we met he was working with hospitals and looking at cancer cures, then he got into nursing homes and building retirement villages.

In about 1995, Ted approached me because he had some people trying to harm him (something about money). So Mario Condello and I flew to Sydney and met a bloke there who could help resolve the issue. I told Ted it would cost $60000 to make the problem go away, the Sydney bloke saw to it, and the three of us got $20000 each for our troubles.

Ted was delighted. 'You've got an eye and ear contract', he told me.

'What does that mean?' I said.

'You are my eyes and ears. All I want you to do is listen and watch—anything you hear about me, you have to come and see me.'

He paid me a retainer, which was beautiful.

As Ted's business grew, he began getting a lot of pressure from the unions, so one day he approached me again looking for help. I brokered a few big deals with the unions for him, involving pay agreements and site allowances—they were very favourable and saved him a lot of money. He was impressed, and the next minute he raised my payment from $4400 to $6600 a month.

So I worked as Ted's 'eyes and ears' (he obviously had a few enemies) and I kept my ear to the ground—anything I heard about him I reported back. And I looked after all his union problems. This continued until the building royal commission in 2001, when I had to give evidence, and my name and Primelife's got dragged through the mud—and Ted got the sack.

It was the typical thing: a European (he was Dutch) trying to fight the blue bloods of a town. I mean, what hope did he have? None. You're talking about Ron Walker and Robert Champion de Crespigny. They had bought into his business and finished up on the board of directors. And they discovered Ted was paying me money—in cash— and saw it as an angle to throw him out. I never understood why they sacked him; he was great at what he did. [*Walker is a former federal treasurer of the Liberal Party, former Melbourne lord mayor, successful businessman, chairman of the Australian Grand Prix Corporation,*

chairman of Fairfax Media, and publisher of titles including The
Australian Financial Review, The Age *and* The Sydney Morning
Herald. *De Crespigny was educated at the elite Melbourne Grammar
School and became a partner in a major chartered accounting business.
He founded a goldmining company that was enormously successful,
and he was named Australian Businessman of the Year in 1993. They
purchased about a 10 per cent stake in Primelife, which was a pretty big
business—it had around six thousand residents living in fifty-odd aged
care and nursing homes. The unfair dismissal case revealed remarkable
boardroom intrigue: Primelife board meetings were secretly filmed
by Sent's closest associate; many company phone calls were secretly
recorded. The case heard that Walker and de Crespigny had personally
investigated $230 000 of cash payments to Gatto, and they thought that
Sent's 'chequered history' spoiled the company's credibility. Ultimately,
after Sent was dismissed, both Walker and de Crespigny sold their
holdings at a profit.]*

I appeared in the Supreme Court and was cross-examined as
a witness, which again dragged my name and finances into the
open. I had probably saved Primelife millions of dollars through the
different agreements I managed to negotiate. Ted said the same thing
in the Supreme Court. But at the end of the day, Primelife was a
public company and he was paying me under the table. He thought
he could do what he wanted; that was the problem. He did nothing
wrong—it was for the benefit of the company—he just should have
done it out in the open. [*Sent explained the cash transactions to* Age
reporter David Elias in 2003:

> *We used Mick Gatto to deal with the unions on our building
> projects. That was known because Gatto was mentioned in
> the Cole Royal Commission as a contractor to Primelife. He
> insisted on cash. He doesn't take cheques. Our office mislaid
> some of the invoices and asked for replacements. They were*

supplied and now it is being said they are false. They are not
false. As for cash irregularities, when did cash become illegal
tender?]

Ted was unlucky. He was paying me cash (and the cash was at
my request). It cost Ted a fair bit of money to fight that case, and in
the end he lost. He thinks my colourful background didn't help. It's
probably true. He rings me from time to time. These days he's trying
to build up a new nursing home business.

I suspected my court appearance would hit the papers, but I
didn't care. I wanted to do the right thing by Ted, but unfortunately
the result didn't go his way.

I actually bumped into Ron Walker in Bourke Street one day after
the case, and I said, 'Hello, Ron, how are you?'

He looked, and said, 'Oh, hello'.

Then he realised who I was and he shot off. But there's no bad
blood there. I saw him again in a restaurant on a recent visit to
England, but I didn't get a chance to say hello. I will next time.

The day after my court appearance, a story appeared in the *Herald*
Sun claiming I had threatened the life of a secretary of the Electrical
Trades Union, Dean Mighell. The story was rubbish, and denied by
all involved, including Dean. (Dean is a good union leader and I like
him. The country should be run by someone like him, because he
has the interests of the people at heart.) But it dragged me into the
spotlight again.

The allegations came from Kerry Milte, a former Commonwealth police officer and a trouble-maker. He thinks he is super-intelligent, and manages to wheedle his way into things. We have a history where he led me up the garden path over criminal charges, which caused me a lot of problems. I don't trust him or like him. The police chief commissioner Christine Nixon employed him as a consultant and, in the end, all he did was cause her a heap of embarrassment. [*In June 2008*, The Australian's *multiple Walkley Award–winning journalist Gary Hughes wrote a damning piece about Milte, which said, in part:*

> *Victoria's police corruption watchdog has found Chief Commissioner Christine Nixon allowed herself to be manipulated by a notorious self-promoting 'Mr Fixit' into establishing a secret taskforce to investigate his supposed inside information about organised crime.*
>
> *Ms Nixon even allowed the informer, former federal police officer and barrister Kerry Milte, to nominate the officers he wanted to work with him on the taskforce, including a corrupt detective later jailed for dealing drugs to Melbourne's underworld during the Gangland War.*
>
> *The taskforce, codenamed Operation Clarendon, quickly ran off the rails and spent most of its time working on investigations aimed at promoting Milte's business interests as a security consultant.*
>
> *An investigation by Victoria's Office of Police Integrity found that Milte, who was later convicted of improperly obtaining information from the force's confidential computer database, also tried to gather information for the corrupt detective about the investigation into his drug dealing.*
>
> *The detective, Senior Sergeant Wayne Strawhorn, was jailed for a minimum of four years in 2006 for selling drugs*

to underworld identity Mark Moran, part of the Moran family crime clan, who was later killed.

Milte pleaded guilty in October 2005 and December 2006 to charges of procuring the disclosure of confidential information from Victoria Police's LEAP database.]

Milte had been interviewed by police and told them I'd threatened Dean and, among other rubbish, said Elite Cranes was funded by Mafia money. (It was funded by a bank loan, and I can guarantee that the books have been examined with a microscope by the tax department.) I was furious. I immediately saw Robert Richter, who I often consult. We talked, and decided I had to defend myself and Elite Cranes. There was no option. So together we wrote out a statement.

'Organise a press conference and just read this out', he said. 'That's it. Don't answer any questions.' So that's exactly what I did.

The press conference was called at Elite, and I walked out with my partner, Mat, and read the statement. It said, in part:

> I have had a colourful past, but I always thought our system of justice and common fairness required that if someone with a colourful past decides to go straight, it is something to be encouraged, rather than sabotaged.
>
> It almost seems as if some people in the media do not want people to go straight, or just want them to try, and fail. Well I did try—and I did so successfully—and I intend to continue to do so.
>
> I am not interested in false rumours and smears designed to hurt my lawful interests and circulated with impunity. The people who do so are cowards. If those making allegations against me have any decency, let them make the allegations publicly so I can take legal action

to protect both my family and my business, which is completely legitimate. Otherwise, they should leave me and my family to get on with life.

[*The press conference was the top story in evening television news bulletins, with anchors describing it as 'extraordinary' and 'bizarre'.*]

I had been working hard to keep my head down. But it seemed that whatever I did, I couldn't keep out of the spotlight.

26

RATS IN THE RANKS

Thirty years ago, the old crew in the underworld—and I knew a lot of them—never made a statement to police. Their word was their bond. If they had a secret, they took it to their grave, no matter what. They were all good people; they had a martyr-type belief. The people I worked with in my early days certainly fitted this category—they were very staunch, with strong principles. A lot of their views were similar to mine. My father often told me, 'If you mind your own business, you will never get into trouble', and that included not talking about other people's business. So I learned not to talk about people's business or their activities—and certainly not to the police.

Times, though, have changed, and the Gangland Wars certainly showed that. Plenty of people informed on their mates, and the police did everything in their power to encourage it. All sorts of sweeteners encouraged people to make statements—whether they were telling the truth or not. And some people were 'rewarded' with much shorter jail sentences for getting in first, and giving up others.

In Victoria, the police effectively run the jails, which means they can put enormous pressure on inmates: locking them alone in a cell for twenty-three hours a day, restricting their visits, cutting their contact with the outside world. They know everything that happens in there. Everything's monitored—all the phone calls, people's cells. They put informers with different people, and try to set them up to say things. It's just terrible.

Among the worst are the 'indemnified witnesses', who the police turn into puppets by offering all sorts of benefits if they say what the police want, even when it is a pack of lies. I think informers are the lowest reptiles in this world. I just don't associate with them, if I can help it. I might say 'Hello', but not much else.

One of the worst examples of an informer that I've come across is The Rat. [*His real name cannot be given for legal reasons.*] The Rat was a drug dealer who grew up in Melbourne's northern suburbs. I only met him once or twice and decided I didn't like him. I thought he was a jellyfish on the first day I met him. Spineless. He was just one of those blokes you could never trust. And I was right. He was involved in killing Jason Moran, a horrific murder in front of a vanload of kids. His lawyer told him he would beat the charge, but he decided to roll and become a puppet for the police—and he got a dramatically reduced sentence.

With his new role, The Rat developed a remarkable memory for conversations and events that had taken place years earlier, vividly remembering discussions word for word. He claimed Andrew Veniamin was a close friend who had 'confessed' to him about a series of murders and events. It was just bullshit. Andrew didn't even like The Rat; in fact, Andrew used to call him a rat. Andrew wouldn't have told him anything, because Andrew didn't brag about what he'd done.

The Rat didn't like me because one day I'd asked a friend to give him a call and get him to come and see me in Carlton. The problem was that I'd learned The Rat was throwing my name around in a bid to collect a debt: 'Don't interfere with me—Mick Gatto's behind me. He'll fix you up'. I was furious. I never like people using my name, especially like that. And I didn't like the bloke anyway. He needed to be pulled into line.

'Don't throw my name around', I told him. 'I don't like you and I'm warning you to never use my name again like that.' I nearly belted him, I was that angry, but I didn't. And he left.

Many years later, The Rat talked to the police and wrapped a new story around those events. Because the police have surveillance records—including some phone taps—there is no dispute that the Carlton meeting happened. But there was no context, and The Rat created a fantasy around some real events.

The Rat didn't like me, and probably saw a chance to get even—which the police would have encouraged. I have been under the police microscope for more than a decade, and for some detectives I am a trophy. And that attitude is like a cancer: it spreads, and gets bigger and bigger until more people believe something must be true. I've been interviewed over a couple of matters based on allegations by The Rat, and there is no evidence to back them up—because they are wrong. It is frustrating and annoying that the police pay any attention to this idiot's fantasies, because it wastes their time and they come unstuck. But no doubt he will be in the witness protection program, they'll relocate him, they'll reward him, they'll release him despite the horrific murder—and, at the end of the day, for what?

Another extraordinary example of an informer is 166, who was going to give evidence against Mario Condello. [*The man's real name cannot be given for legal reasons.*] Even though Mario was killed on the eve of his trial, the police still paid 166 the $1 million they had promised him. The bloke was a low-life drug dealer. He gave evidence at Mario's committal, and everyone could see he was lying. He is the lowest form of human being you can possibly think of, yet he was rewarded for it.

Blind Freddy could have worked out that 166 was a rat. He went over to Adelaide to buy some guns for Mario, and he got pinched with them at the train station. There were about twenty guns in the bag—silencers, machine guns and God knows what. The police took them off him and he was never charged. When he came back to Melbourne, he said, 'I told the police I was taking them to the next town to hand them in as part of the gun amnesty'.

'There's something wrong there', I told Mario. 'Don't do anything with him. I reckon he's rolled over.' And I ended up being right.

I wouldn't talk to 166, although he tried pretty hard. I didn't want to speak to him. Mario, however, made the mistake of talking to him, and he was set up. Mario probably would have beaten the charge against him, because 166 was such a liar. But in the end, Mario didn't get the chance to clear his name.

Other key figures in the Gangland Wars became police informers and all got reduced sentences. [*None can be named here for legal reasons.*] They included:

The Driver, who was the first to roll. He was convicted of killing Michael Marshall, and not prosecuted over Jason Moran and Pasquale Barbaro. We wrote to each other in jail. (I talked to everyone, because I wanted to make sure my family was safe on the outside.) I knew he'd rolled—he told me he'd cut a deal so he'd get less than ten years' jail. 'I hope I've done the right thing', he wrote. Some in Carl Williams' crew thought I was the one who got him to roll, but he'd done that long before I spoke to him.

The Runner, who always had a bit of go in him. He was a lone worker, but this time he got involved with people who promised him the best legal defence—and it never happened. They dropped him like a hot potato. So he probably thought he didn't have much choice; other people had rolled so he figured he might as well do the same.

The Veteran, who knew he faced a massive jail sentence, so he did his best to cast himself in the best light. I'd known him for many years (and never liked him), then saw a bit of him while I was on remand for Andrew Veniamin's murder. The Veteran was aggressive and had a bad way about him. He used to blame his friends if he was caught for anything. He was cunning, like a rat with a gold tooth.

Of course, Carl Williams faced severe problems because of these rats. And when it was time for Carl himself to face the music, he was looking for a deal. He got one. In April 2007, when he pleaded guilty in the Supreme Court to three murders (he'd already been convicted of one more), part of the deal was that he wouldn't be charged with any more murders. Also, they wouldn't charge his father, who wouldn't lose his house. It was quite unbelievable.

Then, around Christmas 2008, police took Carl out of jail for a few days. He had a conjugal visit with his girlfriend and God knows what else. I'm sure he's been made a heap of promises. And no doubt, for that, he'll want a reduction in his sentence. Carl got thirty-five years' jail for four murders—and he killed quite a few more people than that. [*Williams is linked to more than ten murders.*] Yet there are rumours his sentence will get a big cut. You have to wonder what the system has come to.

27

MELBOURNE'S *UNDERBELLY*

I first heard about plans for the *Underbelly* television series from John Silvester, the Melbourne journalist who co-authored the books of the same name. John told me a company called Screentime was planning to do a TV show on the Gangland Wars, and asked if I was interested in meeting those involved. I certainly was—I like to keep my finger on the pulse. John told me they would be doing the series regardless, so this was a chance to put my point of view across.

Sometime later, a few people came to my office at Elite Cranes, including Greg Haddrick, one of the producers, and Des Monaghan, the executive producer. I didn't tell them too much, but they kept sucking things out of me and ended up with some useful information that was used in the show. I told them, 'I am happy to consult for a fee, but I am certainly not going to help for nothing'. But in the end I helped them a bit, and I got nothing for it.

Simon Westaway was cast to play my part, and we met over lunch at a Carlton restaurant. He was a good bloke and we had a chat. Afterwards, a couple of friends asked if I'd noticed what he was doing over lunch. 'Whatever you did, he did', they said.

'What do you mean?'

'When you were picking your teeth with a toothpick, the way you do, he was doing the same. When you drank, he grabbed the glass and drank the same way you do. He was trying to imitate you.'

I hadn't noticed.

That afternoon I made a few inquiries about Simon and discovered he was an ex-copper, which, to me, meant there was no way he could play my part. So that night I rang him. 'Mate, is it true that you used to be a copper?'

'Yes. That was twenty years ago.'

'Well, you can't play my part', I said. 'You are from the other side of the fence.'

'I am a good actor, Mick', he said. 'I promise you, I will make you proud.'

I wasn't convinced and told him I would be ringing Des Monaghan and letting him know. But I thought about it overnight, and decided, 'It's really not up to me who plays my part'. I knew there was a fair chance I could get him moved if I rang Des, but I didn't make the call.

The next morning I rang Simon. 'Just do the best you can for me', I said.

And he did a great job—he made me look very respectable and honourable, although I'm a more happy-go-lucky bloke than he portrayed—and we ended up mates.

One of those in my network of contacts is Eddie McGuire, who was running Channel Nine at the time. It was Eddie's idea to fund *Underbelly*—without him it wouldn't have got off the ground. I'd met Eddie many years earlier, and I like him. Every time I see him somewhere he comes over and says hello, and has a chat—no matter who he is with. Not long ago I saw him at Melbourne's tennis centre with former Victorian premier Steve Bracks. And he waved and came over to shake my hand and say hello. Considering the position Eddie is in, and my high profile and notoriety, I thought it was good form.

During the production of *Underbelly*, I was updated on what was going on, particularly about my character's involvement—and a couple of times I grew concerned about what was happening. In one planned scene, Mario was going to threaten people who owed money and come out owning several car parks. My children own a car park each, which I bought for them years ago, and I didn't want them to watch *Underbelly* and think I'd stood over someone to get them. (I paid cash for them and it's all documented—even the taxman has gone through the paperwork.) They also planned two versions of the Andrew Veniamin shooting—one of what happened, the other the police version of events, which had me executing Andrew, then firing shots around the room to pretend it was self-defence. I took offence at that. I'd been acquitted, yet they wanted to do that.

I rang Eddie and spoke to him. He made some inquiries and found out those scenes weren't going to be used. I was thankful he made those inquiries.

[*Four months after Carl Williams pleaded guilty to three murders, the filming of* Underbelly *began. It took about fifteen weeks to shoot thirteen episodes. The series went to air on 13 February 2008, but was banned in Victoria because of pending legal trials. Five episodes were screened in Victoria in late 2008, but more legal problems have*

prevented any further episodes being shown. The series was a massive hit in the rest of Australia and dominated television industry awards. The DVD produced enormous sales, except in Victoria, where it was banned from sale.]

Channel Nine asked me if I wanted to go to an advance screening with some other people, but I told them I wasn't interested. 'I'll wait until it's on TV', I said. The reality was I'd already seen the first nine episodes. We had pirate copies well before it went to air.

Not long afterwards, Des Monaghan rang me, worried that pirate copies were floating about in Victoria. 'Mick, there's a heap of pirate copies getting around—do you know much about it?'

'Actually, I do, Des', I said. 'I've put a million copies out on the street myself.'

'What do you mean?'

'Well, you didn't pay me any consultation fees, so I had to make my money somehow—and it's going great.'

It wasn't true, but for a long time Des thought it was.

Someone, though, was making a heap. They were selling the whole series for $100, but when people got home and watched it, there were only nine episodes—when they got to episode ten it was blank.

Funnily enough, about this time Simon Westaway came to Melbourne and popped in for lunch.

'Have you seen the series yet?' I asked him.

'No, I have only seen the first couple of episodes; that's all they've released in Sydney.'

I grabbed a bag from under the table—there were about fifty copies in there—and gave him a DVD of the 'whole series' (without the last four episodes). He couldn't believe it. 'Where did you get that?'

'Don't worry about it', I said.

We had a good laugh about that. He took it back to Sydney and watched the first nine episodes. He couldn't believe that he'd been one of the lead actors in the show, and somehow we'd seen the series first.

I watched the whole series in a day. I was glued to it. It was pretty funny to watch because I was involved and knew so many of the players. Some of it was accurate—but they added a lot and glossed it up for TV. Much of it wasn't true, with some parts blown out of proportion. They threw in some murders that just weren't related and created relationships that didn't exist—they didn't let the truth get in the way of a good story. But while some things were off the mark, it all looked good.

I actually took offence at a few aspects, especially with Mario Condello and the money side of things. They had a story where some kid borrowed money, couldn't meet the payments and killed himself. Then Roberta (Carl Williams' wife) had a go at Mario over it. It was just bullshit. None of it happened. The kid didn't exist. And if Roberta had done that to Mario, he would have had a go at her.

In the first episode, they introduced the Carlton Crew—me, Mario Condello, Alphonse Gangitano, Graham Kinniburgh plus Lewis, Mark and Jason Moran—meeting at a football ground. That was rubbish from the start. There was no Carlton Crew. This group, and the term, were invented by a journalist or the police to try to show there were two factions fighting each other. That just wasn't the case. I spent all my days with Ron Bongetti, a pensioner in his seventies. If anyone was the Carlton Crew, it was me and Ron. Small crew, really. I rarely saw Lewis, and hardly ever spoke to Jason or Mark—they all ran their own races. The meetings shown never took place. In fact, I can't remember a single time when all those people sat down at a table together. I don't know if we ever did that. I had plenty of lunches with Graham when Lewis called in—but never Jason. I never got along with Jason; I didn't like his arrogant, fiery attitude. Perhaps we all sat down together at Jason's thirtieth birthday, but I'm not even sure of that—and that would have been with many other people, too. So those meetings were all nonsense.

What I did appreciate, though, was the fact that I was never linked to drugs during the series. I'd told the writers from day one that if they linked me to drugs I'd be furious. And they respected that. Whenever drugs came up, I was off screen.

The most brilliant part of the show for me was Vince Colosimo's portrayal of Alphonse Gangitano. In two or three scenes I couldn't tell whether it was Alphonse or Vince. He was the best in the cast.

In the first episode, he killed Greg Workman, went home, had a shower and went upstairs to bed.

His wife, Virginia, asked, 'Why did you have a shower down in the laundry?'

He replied, 'Go back to sleep, Virginia', and put his shades on. He was a dead ringer for Alphonse. You could not tell the difference. It was really unbelievable.

As for the others, Carl Williams' actor, Gyton Grantley, did well. He looked like Carl and was pretty close, although Carl's a bit dopier than that. Andrew Veniamin came across a lot better than he actually was. Friends who watched the show said Andrew was likeable, but he wasn't like that—he was very jealous, aggressive and ambitious. Damian Walshe-Howling, who played the part, did a good job, but gave the character too much charisma.

Graham's portrayal wasn't bad, although they should have found someone like Gene Hackman to play the role, like he did in the movie *Enemy of the State*. That was Graham. But they got his wife wrong—they had an old woman play her. She did a good job, but in real life Graham's wife is a beautiful, elegant-looking lady. The bloke who played Lewis Moran looked like him, although Lewis was a bit bigger than him. Overall, most of the actors were very good.

The girl who played Roberta Williams did really well, although she was nothing like Roberta. I've met Roberta a few times since the show went to air—she's asked me for help and support. And she's got balls. She has driven in, uninvited, wanting to see me at Elite Cranes.

'Not long ago you tried to get me killed, and now you want me to help you?' I said.

'Oh, don't be like that', was her reply. And she laughed.

She's a single mother trying to raise a family and I'm a bit of a softie. I shouldn't be, but I am, and I've tried to assist where I can. She's got a lot of dash—more dash than Carl ever had. Roberta really should have been a bloke.

Underbelly propelled me into the public spotlight like nothing before. Prior to that I'd had bits and pieces of publicity, but the general public didn't really know me. Once *Underbelly* was out, I couldn't go to a wedding, a funeral, a sporting event, a dinner, without someone recognising me. If I sat quietly at a café someone would come up and ask for a photo or autograph. So I don't go out too much— I stay within my own group—but when I do go out, it always seems to happen.

Even travelling overseas—in Rome and Lebanon—I've been asked for an autograph. It seems everybody knows me, wherever I go.

People walk by and they look back and say, 'It's him'. I see it every day of the week. I don't worry about it and try to ignore it. If someone wants a photo, or whatever, I don't knock them back. I would rather be left alone, living in the shadows. But thanks to *Underbelly* that's not going to happen any more.

28

PROBLEM-SOLVING

For many years I've been a problem-solver—mediating and fixing disputes. Since the mid-1990s, much of that work has been with unions, fixing various industrial problems, and that continues. But there's plenty of other work. Every week I get calls from people wanting me to fix corporate disputes, money issues, marital problems (I try to stay away from those) and business partnership break-ups.

I do a lot of mediation work with long-time friend John Khoury and we have established a reputation for solving what are seen as intractable problems. John is especially successful in mediations because he is a great thinker who works things out very quickly. There have been cases which I thought were impossible to settle, and he's got them over the line. It's all done amicably. Everyone shakes hands in the end, and the lawyers tidy it up. These days we do a lot of corporate mediations, with our clients including public companies, individuals, solicitors, hoteliers and builders.

A good example was a dispute between three partners over a multi-million-dollar Melbourne hotel. Each partner employed lawyers and the dispute dragged on and on, then headed into the courts. By the time we became involved, the three partners had spent about $800000 on legal fees. We organised round-table meetings and resolved it. It went back to court and the Supreme Court judge involved said, 'Whoever did this ought to be congratulated'.

In many cases lawyers stretch out the dispute as long as they can—they're making great money. We come in, and once we've solved the problem we tell the lawyers, 'You've had a good run; this has all been settled now. Now you do what your client wants you to do'. Not surprisingly, the lawyers don't like that.

When it comes to negotiations, my reputation helps. In some cases, if I ring someone and say 'It's Mick Gatto', they nearly collapse. People think I've got two heads because of all the publicity. When they meet me they realise I'm a pretty down-to-earth bloke. Nine times out of ten we settle something simply by getting people together.

The most important part of any mediation is to settle as quickly as possible, to reach a happy medium where everyone is content. In most cases, commonsense prevails. Sometimes, though, a dispute doesn't settle. There have been plenty of cases that were just too hard: we couldn't settle them. This is especially true when companies have gone under and blatantly robbed someone by, for example, moving assets. But we have a pretty good strike rate.

[*In late March 2008, the Melbourne stockbroking firm Opes Prime collapsed and was placed into the hands of administrators. About twelve hundred investors had entrusted their shares to the stockbroker, which had in turn borrowed money from the ANZ Bank—and when Opes collapsed, the ANZ recouped its money by selling the shares. The investors, many of whom did not realise they could lose their shares, lost about $500 million—and promptly wanted to know where the 'missing' money had gone.*]

Within days we were engaged by a Melbourne-based Singaporean. He had about $20 million tied up in it and wanted to know if any of the money was in Singapore—there were key Opes Prime figures based there—and if it was worth pursuing. He also wanted to know who, if anyone, had ripped him off. He agreed to pay all our expenses, including first-class flights and hotels, so we set off.

We flew to Singapore on 8 April 2008. [Underbelly *was part-way through its screening.*] That morning, journalist Mark Hawthorne wrote a story in *The Age* saying I was flying to Singapore to pursue the Opes Prime money trail. One of the boys had leaked it to the media. And journalists started calling my phone—so I told them what time I'd be at the airport.

When I picked up John on the way to the airport, I was wearing a new *A-Team* t-shirt that I'd bought a few days earlier—he said he'd just bought one too, so I persuaded him to put it on as a joke. We picked up my partner, Mat Tomas, who had some other business in Singapore at the same time, but unfortunately no *A-Team* t-shirt. I hadn't told Mat the media might be at the airport, so when we walked in he was stunned. There were TV cameras and reporters everywhere, and they followed us to the check-in counter.

We were trying to be as discreet as possible so we could get on with our job. But once we landed in Singapore, the media were there to greet us. When they asked what we were doing, John said, 'We're not here for the noodles'. We were followed from the airport to our hotel, where we set about finding those involved. But they already knew we were coming because of the media publicity—and they were terrified. They had been spooked by one journalist and thought we were going to harm them and their families. We had to call and assure them that wasn't going to happen. They were in Hong Kong and Macau, and we asked them to fly to Singapore to meet us. After some initial resistance, they agreed. We met in a room at a hotel of their choosing—we were being followed by reporters (and police), so it took some arranging to lose the media pack.

On 10 April, we met with Jay Moghe, Gordon Brown and Raj Maiden, who were all involved with Opes Prime. They were very nervous and keen to help us. They already had a whiteboard ready— and we had a long chat, going right through events. We wanted to know where the money had gone. They explained, and we taped the conversation. It went for about three hours. (I asked one of them why they were so worried about meeting us. He said he'd looked me up on Google.)

We were happy in the end—they convinced us there was no money left and they were not involved. They were just puppets for the guys who were operating Opes Prime. Personally, they had no money. They were battling: they couldn't even pay their rent. So they were free to go.

After the meeting we arranged to have a photograph taken with them, because when we left Melbourne people had doubted us. Some commentators said we wouldn't get anywhere near the directors, we'd learn nothing, that the trip was a stunt. And within forty-eight hours we had a comprehensive picture of what had happened, from those at the top. That was what our client wanted us to do—find out what had happened and establish if these blokes had anything to do with it. And we delivered.

We also found out where their properties and other assets were. And the next moment the liquidator grabbed everything. They thought we were going to take all the cars and other assets in Singapore (and everywhere else).

It seems the Singapore police had the same idea, too. After we checked in at the airport and began a bit of duty-free shopping, we felt a tap on the shoulder. It was the Singapore organised crime police; they were hard-nosed. They took us downstairs to a cordoned-off area—we were escorted by commandos with machine guns—and told us to sit down and not move. They checked us and our bags; they said they were looking for cash and cheques. No doubt the Victorian police had asked them to do it. It was a bit of fun and games. They were a little aggressive at the start, probably because we didn't understand what they were talking about. Eventually they escorted us back to where they picked us up, and we continued our shopping.

On landing in Australia, I got the usual treatment. At Customs, everyone else goes this way; I go that way. I just know where to go now: I don't even bother getting in the line. I just go that way. The three of us were searched and delayed—they took my phone for half an hour, obviously downloading everything on it. They also asked if we had any cash or cheques, then let us go. We walked out, into the media glare again. The television reporters asked, 'Where are the bags of money?' They thought it was a bit of a joke. But we got the job done and the results we needed.

When we got back we also spoke to the official receivers. They were impressed we'd tracked down the directors and found the assets. They also said we had fast-tracked everything they did, including seizing assets. People were coming out of the woodwork, handing in their cars.

All those investors who had money tied up in Opes Prime should thank us, because we sped up the process—including the final settlement—by making the receivers grab the assets quickly, possibly before they disappeared.

We received a lot of calls from people wanting our help to get their money back, but we knew we couldn't do any more for anybody. The liquidators were heavily involved and it was headed towards a preferential payment outcome. We could have taken a fee from people, but we would have been robbing them. That's not how we work.

Ten months later, in February 2009, John Khoury and I flew to London to mediate an international mining deal. It involved Cape Lambert, a big mining company in Western Australia, and a dispute that was heading for the Western Australian Supreme Court. The dispute involved the ownership of a parcel of shares worth about $17.5 million, and a group of shareholders that included one of the world's richest men, Roman Abramovich. He is well known as the owner of London's Chelsea Football Club.

This was a dispute that was unfixable—until we got involved. Again, it was a matter of letting commonsense prevail, seeking a speedy solution and taking the matter out of the lawyers' hands. It has now been fixed. [*A report in* The Age *in June 2009 by journalist Mark Hawthorne summed it up well:*

> *Mick Gatto has helped negotiate a peace deal between Perth company Cape Lambert Iron Ore and major shareholders billionaire Roman Abramovich and British-based Mick Shemesian.*
>
> *Gatto and business associate John Khoury, under the banner of company Arbitrations and Mediations, flew to London for a secret meeting at The Mayfair hotel to help with a peace deal between the warring parties.*
>
> *The meeting at The Mayfair was called by Romanian-born businessman Frank Timis—who has business ties with all the parties, but does not own a stake in Cape Lambert—to try to avoid a messy legal battle in the Supreme Court of Western Australia.*
>
> *Former Shemesian business partner Brett Matich had obtained an injunction from the Supreme Court to stop his old mate selling or voting his Cape Lambert shares.*
>
> *Gatto confirmed Arbitrations and Mediations had helped broker the peace deal. 'Arbitrations and Mediations has gone*

global, you might say', Gatto said. 'If there is a problem that needs sorting out, it doesn't matter where it is. If you fly us there, we'll fix it.'

Cape Lambert is controlled by executive chairman Tony Sage, owner of the Perth Glory A-League soccer club.

Russia's Evraz, controlled by oil and gas billionaire Roman Abramovich, owns about 16 per cent of the company. According to Forbes *magazine, Abramovich is the fifty-first richest person in the world with a US$8.5 billion fortune. He also owns Chelsea Football Club in England. Shemesian's Hong Kong–based Power United owns a 10.5 per cent stake in Cape Lambert.]*

29

LAST MAN STANDING

I was lucky to make it through the Gangland Wars, which claimed the lives of some of my closest friends. I survived the paranoia and lunacy created by those drug dealers who were using too much of their own product. And the main reason I lived was that I had nothing whatsoever to do with drugs. If I had been affiliated with drugs in any way, shape or form, I believe I would have been killed. But I'm still alive.

What has annoyed me—and still does—are suggestions that I was on one side of a 'drugs war'. I have never dealt drugs and am strongly against them, especially the powders and the tablets. It's something inbuilt with me. I've been against drugs all my life. A lot of people around me were involved, but I always shied away from drugs. I always had the belief that if I dealt drugs, my kids would end up on them. It comes back to haunt you.

I've been approached many times to get involved. Even in the days of the Two-Up, people would come and say, 'Mick, are you interested in buying some heroin? We can get it for the right price'. And I would throw them out of the joint. People soon knew where I stood.

When I've been doing it tough the money has been tempting—the amounts are huge in the drugs business—but I've always found another way, and I'm proud about that. You must have certain principles in life, and that's one of my principles. No drugs. Ever.

My inner circle of friends are the same—we are all anti-drugs. It is just a handful of us and we don't get in too much trouble. I don't profess to be an angel—I'd be insulting people's intelligence to say 'I'm squeaky-clean'. I do go outside the boundaries, but it's nothing of any real significance. I think everyone stretches the legalities a little. But I've never been involved in drugs, and never intend to be involved.

I believe the government has a vested interest in the drug business; otherwise, they would legalise aspects of it. If it was legalised, the jails would empty, crime and street violence would drop, overdose deaths would disappear and the police would have much less to do. I firmly believe the government should legalise drugs. If someone wants something badly enough, they'll get it—but where there's no demand, there's no supply. Legalising it would fix a lot of things. But it would also put lots of people—police, prison officers, lawyers—out of work. And that's probably too hard for the government to do.

The best part of my life is my family, although sometimes things become a little scary. One such occasion came in late 2007 when I got a phone call at work. 'Mr Gatto, this is the Royal Melbourne Hospital. Don't be startled, but your son Justin has had an accident.'

'Is he all right?'

'He has hurt his legs, but he will be all right. I don't want to make you panic, but just wanted to let you know. He is here in the Emergency Department at the Royal Melbourne. Just take your time coming out. He is okay.'

I immediately thought they were telling lies, so I shot down there at 100 miles an hour.

Justin was coherent, but he was in a lot of pain. It turned out he had been driving home after a ten-hour shift. He was tired, it was a hot afternoon and he just nodded off. (There was no alcohol in his blood—they tested it.) His car crossed lanes and ran head-on into a four-wheel drive. He must have put his arm up at the moment of impact, because it smashed first into the windscreen and the bone shattered at the elbow. But if he hadn't done that, he probably would have hit the windscreen with his head and suffered massive injuries.

Much of his pain, though, was from his legs, which had been pushed back so hard by the car's dashboard that they had come out of his pelvis. A surgeon came down and said the legs had to be put back within twelve hours, so Justin was taken for emergency surgery.

When something is wrong, such as one of the kids are sick, we always turn to God for help, and we did that day. (While I believe there's a God and there's something after death, I don't believe in the Church, or that you have to pray every week. The Catholic Church is the richest business in the world.)

The surgery went well, and Justin was put into a ward to recover. He complained about a stomach ache, but the staff put it down to the medication and soreness. It ended up being a blood clot on his lungs, and his lungs collapsed. He was rushed to intensive care and was lucky to survive—it was touch and go for a while. He spent a week in intensive care, then two months in hospital recovering from his injuries.

Sometime later I bumped into the surgeon, who said the week after Justin's accident a man the same age with almost identical leg injuries had come in—and died on the operating table. 'Your son is a strong boy and he is very, very lucky to have survived', the surgeon said.

In 2008, my eldest son, Damien, married Fiona, who is a gorgeous girl. Their fifteen-week-old son, Dominic, was at their wedding. It was a great day.

I know my grandson as Little Mickey Blue Eyes. He's a beautiful boy and he's big—he's going to be a giant. I'm Dominic Gatto too, but he will be taking a completely different path to me. His parents are both very level-headed—I expect he will have a good education, a good future and get into a different line of work from his grandfather! The three of them lived with us for the first year of his life, while his parents built their house, which was wonderful. We especially missed Dominic when they left. He warmed our hearts.

In February 2009, I walked my daughter, Sarah, down the aisle—twice. She married Regan, whose parents are Greek, once in a Greek church and once in a Catholic church: two weddings on the same day. My son-in-law is a lovely, honest, bright bloke—he works for me at Elite (like most of my family do). They are a beautiful couple.

I ring my mother every day—she lives in her own home—and see her most weeks. We speak a mix of English and Calabrian (a dialect most Italians don't understand).

I also have two beautiful young children from an affair some years ago. I love them and will support them until the day I die. They have stayed out of the limelight, and I intend to keep it that way.

The media attention that I have copped since *Underbelly* went to air has been phenomenal, and shows no sign of easing. If I have lunch at a new restaurant or go to a funeral, or even if my neighbour sells his house, it makes news. It's ridiculous.

In June 2008, however, I encouraged media attention to support former boxing triple world champion Jeff Fenech prepare for a fight against Azumah Nelson. I had no financial stake in the event; I was supporting a friend and supporting boxing. So Jeff used my gym at home for training, and we did some media together (including a funny segment with *A Current Affair*'s Martin King, where I got to punch a journalist—gently—without any comebacks).

Just before the Fenech fight, I had an on-air discussion with Derryn Hinch. He had been giving me a spray on radio and someone rang John Khoury to tell him. John and I were having a coffee in Bourke Street and John said, 'Why don't we ring him?' John rang, got through to Hinch, then passed the phone to me.

I was going to have a casual chat to him—What have I done? Why are you giving me a burn? One thing led to another, and he got my blood boiling. I told him what I thought of him. I didn't hold back. Some people interpreted that as a threat—it wasn't. Hinch had gone on national television saying he had cirrhosis of the liver and possibly liver cancer from a lifetime of heavy drinking, and his doctors told him he didn't have long to live. He was a very sick man.

In the end it was pretty funny. One outcome was that the media wanted to talk to me about the Hinch conversation, and Jeff Fenech's agent, Max Markson, offered to help. Max is a great bloke, and now my agent, too. Max teed up an interview with *A Current Affair*, who paid me an appearance fee. (I gave it all to the Royal Children's Hospital.) So, in the end, Derryn Hinch finally did something useful in his life, by helping raise money for sick kids.

Giving to charity has always been important to me, especially the Royal Children's Hospital. Often people ask for financial help, and there are few I refuse. I usually help people who come out of jail, because those first few weeks out can be tough. I'll give them two, three or five grand, and I never ask for it back. But it finds its way back one way or another. It is also important to support close friends. In 2008, I held a fundraiser for a friend who was facing a murder charge so he could get the best possible legal representation.

My attitude to money is 'easy come, easy go', and I think it's made me a better person, especially helping people in trouble. It's something I've tried to instil in my children. I've also tried to teach them to treat people the way they treat you. It's been my philosophy for a long time. You will hear good and bad about someone, but it makes no difference what you hear; you treat them the way they treat you. If someone treats you like shit, then you do the same; if they treat you with respect, then respect them doubly.

In 2002, I went with my two sons and one of their friends to the FIFA World Cup in Japan. Every day we caught the train and there was a bloke on the railway bridge, begging—he had no legs. And every day I gave him money. On the last day, I went up to this bloke and gave him all the money I had left. I said, 'Take that. I am going back to Australia'. I was trying to explain because he couldn't quite understand. He started crying, the poor bugger, tears streaming out of his eyes. He grabbed my hand—and the kids were quite taken aback by it. They couldn't believe this man, who I'd never properly met, was crying.

In 2008, I had a gambling purple patch and was up about $800 000. (Not long afterwards I lost all the money again.) Everything I backed seemed to win. And I thought, 'Bugger it, I'm going to take a few of the old boys who have never been out of Australia on a holiday'. So I rounded up about half-a-dozen of these friends, they each got a passport and we got on a plane for Hong Kong. There were about thirty of us altogether. We took a ferry to Macau and stayed at the Venetian, which is a magnificent hotel. Everyone was chauffeured around in limos, taken to the best restaurants, karaoke bars and other places. All the old boys had the time of their lives, and I was happy to do that. It gave them a bit of a thrill. It was money well spent.

On 7 February 2009, severe bushfires swept through Victoria, killing more than one hundred and seventy people. My friend Dave 'The Rock' Hedgcock was caught up in the fires. It was a hot day and he drove from the city to fix the broken air-conditioning at his home near Kinglake, where his daughter-in-law, grandson (aged six) and granddaughter (aged fourteen months) were staying. About twenty minutes after he got there the fire-front hit, and he scrambled to get the family out. They managed to get away, but it was a very

close-run thing, and Dave told me about some of the horrific sights he witnessed. His house was destroyed.

A week later, I was talking with friends about how we could help. One of those there was *Herald Sun* photographer Peter Ward, who has been a friend for many years. Next minute, Peter found a bucket, put a sign on it and took a photo—which appeared in the paper, saying I was holding a fundraiser with the aim of collecting $1 million.

Once it was in the paper, I was under the whip. I went through my telephone index and asked everyone to support me by buying a table for ten people for $10000 (even though they were a little bit expensive). The fundraiser attracted some criticism, but I expected that. Whatever I do in life is controversial. A lot of people want me to fail, rather than succeed. They want me to look bad, or look like a crook trying to rectify his reputation. It doesn't bother me. The people who know me know the truth.

Anyone who was breathing would have wanted to help those affected by the fires, and, rather than giving money to the overall Red Cross Appeal, I decided we should help those at the front line—the firemen. Because I'd grown up next to the fire station and I knew a lot of their stories, it struck a special chord in me. I'd had a lot of fun with the firemen, and also seen the tragic side—a few fell through roofs and died over the years.

We had a lot of help putting the event together and on the night, 23 April 2009, about eleven hundred people came, including volunteer firefighters. They were provided with a superb dinner, with wines, and with some fantastic entertainment, including bands, comedians and a magician. Three weeks later I presented a cheque for $896825 to the Country Fire Authority's chief Neil Bibby. It was a proud moment.

When I was young I rode a motorcycle. The first time I came off was going down a hill—I accidentally put on the front brake and did a somersault, and the bike nearly landed on top of me. The second time, it was wet and the front wheel hit a tram track in the city. The bike skidded onto the other side of the road and I finished up underneath a semi-trailer that was stationary at the lights. I was badly grazed, but no bones were broken. I vowed I would never ride a motorbike again.

Then, in 2005, after being acquitted of murder, I had a ride and it rekindled the beautiful sense of freedom (or perhaps it was a midlife crisis). I rode a 250 c.c. for a while, then upgraded to a Harley-Davidson Springer, and I love it. When it's a sunny day I jump on and really enjoy it. It's great fun.

I've also been taking flying lessons in a helicopter. My first lesson was memorable. I went up in a little bubble chopper—I just squeezed in with the pilot—and, as we hovered at 1200 feet, I said to the pilot, 'What would happen if the motor stopped?'

'I'll show you', he said, and he turned the engine off.

The chopper just hovered down and landed in a paddock. I couldn't believe it. The rotor keeps turning at the angle it's on.

'I'll never ask that again', I thought.

For many years I have been the subject of police investigations, and I don't expect that to end. Sadly, the authorities suspect that I'm involved with the Mafia. They believe that because I come from Calabria and I have a criminal record, I must be involved in the Mafia. It's just nonsense. The Mafia doesn't exist in Australia. There's a friendship and bond between Italians who came here from the old country, which is great. They go to funerals and weddings, and show a lot of respect. Some Italians in the community are very influential; if there's a problem, you talk to them and they rectify it. But it's not the Mafia. The only Mafia in this country are the politicians in Parliament House—they can change laws overnight.

I remain security-conscious, and will for the rest of my days. I tell few people my plans. The house has security cameras and a high security fence, which required a special permit from my local council.

For some reason, I'm banned from all Australian casinos and racecourses—and I don't understand why. I was found not guilty of murder, yet I'm still punished. Worse, there is no right to appeal. While I wasn't a big fan of racetracks and didn't go often, I miss the casino. Yet the ban has done me a lot of good—I have saved a huge amount of money and directed my energy into my family and my businesses.

I still manage to bet, though, and sometimes I do well. One Sunday in 2008, I made some bets through a friend called Tony—he knew a bookmaker who happily took the bets. Luck didn't run my way during the afternoon: I was down about $150 000 near the end of the day.

About 6.30 p.m., I rang Tony. I wanted $5000 to win on a horse called Victory Prize, racing in Hong Kong. The reason I picked the horse was simple: I looked at the board and it was paying $30, so if it won, I'd get $150 000 back and be square. Some bookmakers let the punter choose a particular TAB. The final dividend that TAB pays on a particular horse is what the punter will be paid. I chose UNiTAB.

Tony rang the bookmaker, but he had left his office, where he'd been watching all his screens. Tony couldn't get him. I asked him to give it another try—and Tony got through to the bookmaker's son, who was in the car with his dad, driving home. And he took the bet. Most times a bookmaker will put some of that money onto the TAB where the bet has been placed—in this case on UNiTAB. It lessens the risk, but more importantly it brings down the final payout odds. But the bookmaker was in the car on the way home, and didn't do it.

Race time came and Victory Prize stormed home, winning by five lengths. Best of all, though, was the odds had blown right out and it paid $84.20. So I won $421 000. Once I took away the $150 000, I was $271 000 in front. Tony rang back the bookmaker, who was just shattered. But I never have any problem taking money from a bookie; as far as I'm concerned they are fair game.

At the time, I'd just ordered a new Mercedes. It was a lease car for Elite Cranes. But instead I went and bought it outright. My Victory Prize.

Most days I hear about someone using my name—they claim to 'know' me, are my 'driver' or 'work with' me. My new-found reputation (since *Underbelly*) has made it worse, although it can be to my advantage when I need to get something done; people tend to pay attention. But most of it is nonsense, and I pull it up when I can. It's the cases I don't hear about that concern me: my name can become linked to all sorts of problems without my authority and knowledge. Thankfully, I have a lot of friends around Australia, and they let me know if they hear my name being used.

In 2008, Adelaide property developer Cathy Jayne Pearce (who was apparently once on the *Business Review Weekly*'s Rich List) used my name to try to extract a debt, saying, 'We've got Mick Gatto in the car and we want that money that's owing'. It was nonsense, and the first I heard of it was when a friend rang to tell me. Pearce ended up apologising after the story was aired on *A Current Affair* and *Today Tonight*.

My reputation in the underworld is that I'm fair dinkum—if I say something, you should believe it. I'm straight up and down, and can be trusted. That's been my reputation for a long time and I pride myself on it. I also have a reputation for no nonsense and not taking a backward step. People have learned they can't treat me like a mug. I won't cop it. If someone tries to stand over me or does the wrong thing, they know they will be dealt with. My temper's not quick—it's actually quite slow—but the moment you push the button, God help you.

Again, sometimes my reputation can help. A few years ago I had a visit from a woman I won't name, but she worked with a team of Romanian pickpockets that specialised in robbing people on trams. 'Mick, you wouldn't believe what happened', she said.

'What?'

'We were working on a tram, me and a couple of boys, and picked this woman's purse. We opened the thing up and it was your wife, Cheryle. So we closed the purse and put it back.'

She said they were looking at the credit cards when she said to the boys, 'We can't take this; it's a mate of mine's wife'.

I mentioned it to Cheryle and she said, 'I remember someone bumping into me but I didn't think anything of it'. There are advantages in being known.

One sad aspect of the Gangland Wars is that not only did I lose close friends, I also lost their families. Unfortunately, certain police suggested to the families that I was linked to the murders, including those of Mario Condello and Graham Kinniburgh. It's sickening, and still makes my blood boil, but that seems to be police humour—or a bid to turn people against each other. Mario's family have changed their name and don't talk to me. Sadly, Graham's family don't talk to me either. Hopefully time will change this.

As to my future, that's anyone's guess. If you told me five years ago I'd be writing a book today, I would have laughed. Occasionally I see a clairvoyant to give me tips on the future. I've been doing that since I was young, and now know a couple of good ones. One woman, who I've seen a few times in the past decade, has been spot-on about all sorts of things. It's amazing. But it doesn't tell me everything.

The reality is I take life day by day. If I had thought about my future, I would own half of Carlton because of the money that's passed through my hands—but I'm not that way inclined. I don't care that I didn't save millions in the 1980s and 1990s. I don't want to have a lot of wealth and a lot of money. I'm not ambitious that way. With great wealth comes great headaches. I take life as it comes and cross the bridges as I come to them.

I have my family, my health and a beautiful home. Elite Cranes is in great shape and its future looks bright. As long as my family is all right, everything else—houses, cars, clothes, whatever—works itself out. Today, I've got everything I need. And if I remain the way I am, I, Mick Gatto, will be a very happy man.

ACKNOWLEDGEMENTS

We would like to thank Louise Adler and Foong Ling Kong at Melbourne University Publishing for backing this project and their support along the way; book editor Penny Mansley; Kimberley Nichols for her advice and excellent transcription; Peter Ward for the many, many photographs in this book; Max Markson for his fine work behind the scenes; Guy Grossi for the use of his restaurant for the book launch (and his beautiful food); and those many other people who have been involved in helping put this book together—you know who you are. And most of all we would like to thank our families for their love and support.